In the Company *of* Poets

An anthology celebrating 21 years of
poetry readings at Torriano Meeting House

edited by
John Rety

Hearing Eye
2003

Editor: John Rety

Copy editors: Jennifer Johnson and Susan Johns

Editorial Advisory Group: Sara Boyes, Brian Docherty,
David Floyd, Jennifer Johnson, Dan Kennedy, Christopher Morgan,
Phil Poole and Tom Rubens
MS transcription typist: Anna Robinson

Layout and Design: Emily Johns
Printed by: Aldgate Press, Whitechapel E1

ISBN   1 870841 89 1

*This book has been made possible with the financial assistance of
Arts Council England.*

Hearing Eye

Box 1, 99 Torriano Avenue, London NW5 2RX, UK

e-mail: hearing_eye@torriano.org
website: www.torriano.org

CONTENTS

Introduction

This anthology has been compiled to celebrate a community of poets who have gathered over the past twenty-one years at Torriano Meeting House. This is a small but internationally known cultural space in Kentish Town, North London, where Sunday evening readings have been held since 1982. Many poets and other visitors have commented on its ambience and the pleasure of reading their own work and listening to others in this supportive atmosphere, with pictures on the walls, flowers on the platform and an appreciative audience. As well as the evening's main readers invited from a broad range of literary practice, there are usually a number of 'poets from the floor', who may include full-time poets and also beginners presenting a piece in public for the first time. All these members of the community are represented in this book.

The publishing imprint, Hearing Eye, grew out of these encounters, beginning in 1987 with John Heath-Stubbs' *Cats' Parnassus*, and has since produced some 90 books and pamphlets of poetry. Many of the pamphlets have been the first publication of their authors; others are by well-known writers and translators.

A word on how this book was put together: all those who have been in contact with 'Torriano' recently were invited to send work which was either new or had not appeared in book form. The response was quick, enthusiastic and very generous. An advisory group was established to sift and select and assist with the preliminary work, the amount of which was not foreseen by me. That a small team with a minimum of resources could produce such a large compilation means that the editor is indebted to a number of people, in particular to the designer and to the copy editors, who have done far more work than he has done. Perhaps the best contribution of an editor to such a task is willingness to take responsibility. However, this editor has used his prerogative to include some authors in addition to those who initially offered work.

A great regret is that, as they are no longer living, some of our best poets could not be included within the scope of this book, in particular the editor misses A.C. Jacobs, Adam Johnson, Jean MacVean and Bob Cobbing.

These are difficult times and not only for literature. The act of writing itself has changed. Languages are now in the grip of machines. A thousand years from now a young scholar/poet might chance upon this book and be perplexed to learn that these poems were actually composed in the head and that many of them were written by hand, even with a pen on pieces of paper. What literature or poetry might mean then, I cannot even guess, but for me now, the poems offered here have given much delight and instruction and in the words on the page I often seem to hear the familiar voices of their authors. To all those who have helped to create this book, many thanks.

John Rety
London Spring 2003

DANNIE ABSE

Dog on a Beach

A wanton sunset:
a few isolated, blood-filled clouds
and the golden background
of a Sienese painting.

The holiday-makers have gone home,
the beach empty
except for a motionless dog.

The dog, attentive to the inaudible
world of Eternity, faces
the unfolding, funeral-paced,
incoming waves of night
and begins to howl.

The dog is not sentimental.
His master is not out there
somewhere on the horizon
in a sinking ship.

The dog, motionless,
its jaws lifted,
is howling and howling
at the purpural sky,
at the Sienese paint
falling below the sea, yet again.

SHANTA ACHARYA

City Slickers

Helmeted musclemen gliding on steel escalators
bomb-proof buildings in the City against terrorists.

Space-walking on huge walls of glass,
they examine me as they would any other lass.

Smiling, they take a random walk, unafraid of vertigo
like the stock market index raring to go.

Who said men do not make passes at women with glasses?
Real men do, particularly at women in City offices!

Cubicles, now shatterproof, hold fragile egos.
Men in dark grey suits shuffle in corporate shoes.

Pin-stripe suits come and go, talking of P/E ratio,
top-down, bottom-up methods of the intelligent investor.

As I mend the rules of the old boys' network
and demand my share of the profits of my work

I hit the invisible glass ceiling each time
I stand up for myself as if that was a crime.

A single, Indian female, I am trapped, alas,
in a cage of bomb-proof, shatter-proof glass.

The Jurassic laws in the City continue to spawn
dinosaurs that even Spielberg cannot improve upon.

Next time these helmeted musclemen blow me a kiss,
I will signal to them to rescue a woman in distress.

At The Edge Of The World

After Anish Kapoor's 'creations' at the Hayward Gallery

The queue outside is stretching
like an alley cat, waiting
to prowl inside the crowded gallery,
explore the plugged-holes at the centre
of walls and ceilings. Not enough time,
space for all to experience ways of defining It,
of lending shape, colour, sound, meaning.

Once inside, the world is turned upside down,
inside out, disoriented through double mirrors,
emptied of space funnelling into *arupa*,
untitled, leaving us newly-born, fearful of oblivion.

In the beginning (or is it the end?)
securing myself a discrete position,
I get sucked into my mother's womb,
peering at deep, dark shrines of
my body, her body; our bodies
moving in rhythm to creations
at the vortex, doubly-inverted images,
when I become pregnant, making the world many.

We exchange according to our measure
the open-endedness of things; configuring
a nose, a breast, a man posing in his briefs?
Or something new waiting to be seen.

Imagination turns earth and stone into sky.
In the dark, polished hollow of a marble mummy,
a fleeting spirit appears. A twisting column of light,
I flicker before giving up the ghost.

What You Don't Know

As a child you instinctively know
that there are things you don't know;
you also know that you know of things
that the adults think you don't know.

Growing up is a process of knowing,
of knowing that you don't know;
acknowledging that others might know,
though they don't know that you don't know!

Wisdom comes when you can forget what you know,
when you know that parents, friends, lovers, well-wishers,
even your enemies, your best teachers, don't know;
for what is worth knowing is what you don't know.

Some people are born plain lucky;
they sail through life without knowing
that they don't know, and not knowing
they don't know what is worth knowing
protects them from a lifetime of unknowing.

For most of us there is a price to be paid,
most of us get damaged, more or less, in the process
and end up knowing what is not worth knowing.

TIMOTHY ADES

The Hippopotamus

The sturdy Hippopotamus
inhabits jungles Javanese
where snarl in caverns bottomless
undreamable monstrosities.

The boa hisses and unscrews;
snuffles convulse the buffalo;
the tiger caterwauls. *He* chews,
or slumbers, tranquillissimo.

He fears not kris nor assegai,
he looks at man and stands his ground;
he laughs, when shots from the sepoy
spatter his leather and rebound.

The Hippopotamus and I
have an impenetrable hide.
In armour-plate of certainty
I roam the plains with dauntless stride.

*A poem about a Rhinoceros, translated from
the French of Théophile Gautier (1811-1872)*

JOHN ARDEN

Verses For St Valentine's Day, 2001

written when about to attend a meeting of a senior citizens' action group

The day before Saint Valentine
I'd come to Galway Town
to mix myself in harmony
with many an aged clown

that hobbles and halts and gasps for breath
and staggers upon a stick,
the deaf, the blind, the rheumatoid,
the downright paralytic.

I said to my love of forty-odd years,
'This cannot be for me!
I am no Ancient Mariner
new-crawled from the shrivelling sea.

So what if I'm into my eighth decade?
So what if they have me choking
my daily way through five fierce pills
to stop myself from croaking?'

She laughed: 'Your age is what it might be;
if you don't think it, then you're not.
I'm nearly as old as you.' She laughed
like thorns beneath a pot.

Vexatious laugh, but lovely laugh,
laugh of a woman alive:
she laughed just as I saw her laugh
in nineteen fifty-five.

These aged clowns would never meet
if they didn't think they lived.
Let's go and help 'em stir the soup
of those that have survived.

Let's help 'em stir the peppered soup
and feed it to the nation.
For there shall be no better cooks
than those who've not forgotten.

PAT ARROWSMITH

Slow Motion

Inert, hefty, bed-panned,
Hardly an individual at all…
At last I manage to heave up
Across the sheet and out and down…

Then gingerly, heavily,
Hoist clumsy, fragile limb
Back up precipice,
On to mattress,
Eventually under covers into bed.

Later on post-hip op,
Clicketty clock stutter my crutches
In staccato rhythm.
And staggering on staircase
I linger stick-propped,
Stabilize and stave off vertigo
By staring at my feet,
Stopping, pausing on each separate step.

I go slowly now
But do not mind.
When not scrutinizing lumpy ground
To ensure I do not stumble, tumble,
It's good unhurriedly to look around:
See polished bubbles float
On tiny mirror puddles;
Note green mosaic
Of rain shined ivy leaves.

For why rush and bustle,
Thus hasten fast approaching future?
Why this current greed for speed—
Need to smash sound barriers,
Chop three seconds off some record?
Better to concentrate on here and now,
Leisurely observe what is to hand.

War in Afghanistan

Is this the Old Stone Age revived,
Or, maybe, resurrected Middle Ages,
When our supposed dire enemy,
Bearded, piercing-eyed,
Looking even quite benign,
Like some percipient sage of yore,
Squats concealed in deep caves,
Appears on horseback fleeing over mountains?

No, it is all too here and now:
Computer-aided aircraft slicing skyscrapers;
Massive, not so floral 'daisy cutters'
Wreaking wicked, wholesale revenge;
Soft-sounding deadly 'cluster bombs'
Blasting the innocent, unwary,
To bloody smithereens.

But we must define then expedite
A new non-violent era —
Real 'new world order' —
A future where we, people of the earth,
No longer torture, tear ourselves to pieces,
Cower paralysed with terror
At the prospect of fresh barbarism, battles,
More racial and religious strife,
Even nuclear obliteration.

We must fight for peace and justice now —
Now, before it is too late.

This poem was written for and read at the protest rally outside the Northwood war command centre on 9th December 2001

WANDA BARFORD

Encounter

I met Abraham to-day
walking over a dune
with his goats and his camels,
and I greeted him warmly
in my best Biblical voice.

And he, not at all patriarchal,
said: 'When I left my Sarah
at dawn this morning, she was still laughing.
You see, we'd had three very odd visitors
who insisted she'd soon be pregnant. But at her age?
Besides, I already have a son.

'And I do miss Lot my nephew
who settled in the lush country around Sodom.
Forgive me, I should be enquiring after *your* family.'

But as I was about to tell him
how my grandparents went up in smoke
he vanished... only the tinkly sound
of goat bells hung on the Negev air,
now louder, now softer,
over the undulating sands.

You Left Paris First

And now you've gone —
And half of me's gone too.
We stood on bridges looking at the Seine:
Its barges, bâteaux-mouches, their V-shaped wakes,
And wondered how it could be
We were so in love
At an age as ridiculous as ours —
The curving spine, the sagging skin...

Yet love there was,
As vigorous and strange
As any younger love might be,
And maybe twice as loyal
For all the knowledge of deep hurt,
For all the life already lived.

5 a.m.

I stretched out my hand
To touch if you were there
In real flesh; that I hadn't
Imagined your body-warmth,
The feel of your moulded thighs,
That quick response of tiny kisses
Along my outward-curving back
Smoothly fitting into you.

And yes, you clasped my hand,
Held it like a traveller reaching land
After a voyage longer than it should have been...
And yes our bodies said, yes, these trees,
These skies, these singing leaves
Are ours, the new world of our discovery.

BRUCE BARNES

dis is able

Dis
is able,
dis is able to
say, we are to tear
the labels off who we are.

We are
in the 8th day,
we have gone to Him
cap in hand, asking who
did he make the world for?

He could
slip into the
common place,
and quip that we are
handicapped; but he lends

us His
scrawny,
tireless hands
to make a heaven
of the where we are.

In the
beginning
the word lies broken;
there's someone to sign
as minds and bodies sing

The
first fruit is
im*pear*ment / im*pair*ment
a coming together that denies
the labels their sense or power

Barbers

I watch his hands, an energy of fingers
that welds him to his scissors, and I think
of past barbers in their clipping handfuls:

the last, a squat Italian, snipping
in North London, who spoke, as this one does,
an Esperanto of haircuts, with numbers
tidying up the hairy nouns, 'You want the one'
for a little left on, or 'Zero, yes?'
for follicles and their nothingness.

He had a poster of Roma and one for Spurs,
layered in the crew cut turf, with Ginola,
a Samson among the shorn Philistines.

Mr Hussain motions to the chair.
Falling into his arms is like the old game
of trust. There's a hair's breadth moment that hangs,
light and airborne, slowing in the dust
underneath a white rumpled sheet.
I could be anywhere:

outside in some crowded piazza, scalped
and the skull's blood crying *Perche mi scerpi?*
Non hai tu spirito di pietade alcuno?*

or in another Jahangir Saloon,
with my mop of hair sticky in Mirpur's heat.
As someone else is getting done, I wait
on a cane chair, staring at two photos
tacked to a mud brick wall; they gel
to hold in place _____

a child, his crying diminished by the height
of the barber's chair he's stuck in, clings
to a toy ambulance. No help will come;

he of the quiff is a haircut more
than a doppelganger's. His scented profile
slips out of the chair, out of the frame;
I replace him, wondering how I know
that face? He doesn't tip, but leaves a dust trail
shimmering in the street of barbers...

It's all come off; the untidy locks,
the unreachable wisps at the back
of the neck, are carpeting my toe-caps.
Mr Hussain holds up a hand glass
and does an infinity trick, the mirror
steadying within the wall mirror,
showing an endlessness of ruler straight nape,
and beyond me, in perpetuity,
the flash of some plastic flowers.

I nod. It's O.K. Mr Hussain doesn't have
a price list. I do some mental arithmetic.
So, what would I pay myself...

to be here, with those other men's hairstyles
and this packet of me for the weekend,
in the mid morning sun streaming,
bouncing off the tiles in an Oak Lane shop.
I reckon three or four quid...
three being lucky and four's a leg to stand on.

*From Dante's Inferno: 'Why do you tear at me?
Have you no sense of pity?' Canto XIII lines 35-36.*

MICHAEL BARTHOLOMEW-BIGGS

Say It With...

'What you done wrong then, mate?'
There's perfect rhythm
in a perfect stranger's query
as he sees me on the Essex Road,
one arm full of orange Alstroemeria.
'Well, let's just say I hope it works'
accepts the premise, dodges detail
and colludes with blunt assumptions
marriage is guerrilla war
of floral versus verbal weapons.
I should stretch loose prejudice,
extend his list of peccadilloes:
'I was grumbling at her cooking
to her sister in the shower...'
Or 'I just scratched my boyfriend's face...'

Cheap-shoe streets of shabby pubs
are grimed by quiet pessimism:
wry humour is an easy solvent,
wiping off the surface worst, at best.
Under pavements and all nearby floorboards
things are scuttling
where you wouldn't want to put your hand.

In the butcher's, Mr Hudson beams.
He's as sharp and to the point
as his best boning-knife —
and about as unsurprising:
'You didn't need to bring me flowers.'

Led By The Nose

From a sidestreet garage
a strange damp tang emerges, curling
like a finger switching on a memory.
The last coal merchant operating in N1
is into plastic bags and cash'n'carry;

but coalmen I remember
wore seal-scalp leather caps,
a single flipper hanging down behind
to shield their shoulders from the lumpy cargoes,
like carcasses, they hefted off the lorry
down our side way, twenty at a time
in centrally-unheated fifties Britain.

My Mum, afraid of nothing worse
than workman's language, wanted me indoors
hinting that the white-eyes
had all done time in prison.

She was not the last who tried to demonize
providers of the rough and ready energy
that once fuelled winter fireside society.
Anchored firm as concrete plugs
in nineteen-eighties pit shafts,
redundant coal-hole covers punctuate
the Yorkstone pavement like full stops
hammered by an iron-handed typist
with insufficient care about the shift key.

GERARD BENSON

Dannie Doyle, My Uncle

My thin uncle, was it half a stomach you had,
or a half-measure of intestine?
Whichever. They'd certainly cut you about.
I remember the pile of your cropped hair
under my fingers as I sat on your knee
when you came back from Franco's prison;
you said you'd carved a chess set out of soap.

Ambition brought out the skiver in you
and you deserted London and *Doyle Design*
for the life of an odd-job-man,
later, carpenter at an Art School,
where you made and mended and fixed.
They mounted exhibitions
of your lean and twisted sculptures.

Your jokes came from some alien territory,
quiet, weird, disturbing — but always funny.
You called me 'Dard' (my brother's botched attempt)
long after everybody else had forgotten.
And from the depth of your poverty, you gave me
a magnificent junk-shop early Yeats
for Christmas; my only rare edition.

Age made your visits rarer,
your jokes more desperate.
Grey-bearded, you sat on the stairs.
Cancer had wasted your thinness to nothing.
At your funeral the tape machine misbehaved,
and played *Eine Kleine Nachtmusik* three times
before anyone had the nerve to silence it.

Atkinson

Squat, middle-aged and muscular,
Mr Atkinson walked on the balls of his feet,
vibrated with menace, carried surprise like a weapon.

His voice, whisper or roar, terrified us.
His cold blue watery eyes were windows
to a wilderness of contempt. He kept good order.

His blows to the head were swift,
deadly, often came from behind.
He enjoyed his unpredictability.

Walking at night through fenland,
a tall girl led me. Her hand was ice-like,
her long body was wrapped in a cerement.

Others had seen her. They called her Meg,
Meg of the Marsh, marish Meg,
But as we walked I knew her real name.

With dawn she disappeared. 'We must all regret'
our bland headteacher said, at assembly,
'the sudden and unfortunate demise

of Desmond Atkinson' (Desmond?) 'who gave
so unstintingly of his time and energy
to Bascombe High School.' I looked at Smith.

He winked. Gratefully we sang *Now the day is over*
as Miss Cornell's hands placidly depressed
the yellow piano keys. Atkinson was gone. (Alas!)

I watched Brute Davis, singing along
on the platform, Eyebrows Bambury, mouthing.
At the hymn's close I did not sing 'Amen'.

Angiogram

They lift my gown and pose a strip of paper
across my genitals to affirm my modesty,
anoint my groin with tangy yellow, then cover
me over. They touch my face, talk soothingly.
I am a body, soon to be explored.
A camera and monitors are aligned
for action. Lights. A doctor gives the word,
prepares his gear, then needles me. I'm primed
for invasion. He sends a tube along an artery
until he finds my thunderous heart. The monitors
are showing a weird delta—murky estuary.
The camera arcs and swoops. I hear the doctor's
brief command, and feel hot blood which surges
through heart and head; and thank the lord for nurses.

Bionic

For cardio-thoracic surgery they take a saw
and divide the sternum cleanly in two.

They sever the muscle beneath, and then
wrench the ribcage apart (like a box), when

lungs and heart lie exposed to their scrutiny.
Now begins the more intricate surgery,

the opening of the frozen heart, the incision,
the sewing of the new valve — titanium,

with dozens of stitches, which is why
it takes them so long. Meanwhile you lie

lapped in anaesthetic, while a computer
does the work of heart and lungs. Later

you wake to pain but there are things that are worse,
knowledge for example. Immobility is another curse.

I came to: a plumbing system of tubes and alarms,
plugged into neck, heart, lungs, penis, arms.

There's the rich gush of vomited blood: the mask,
the constant attention. They neither apologise nor ask

but like acolytes white-clad attend the mending
body. In a limbo of anaesthetic, in an unending

dream, the mind travels; while freed from stenosis, fixed
with a metal valve, the aorta lives from one beat to the next.

Get-well cards — funny ones not appreciated; odd scenes,
visitors, the vast ward window, sky, machines.

'I held your heart in my hands,' the surgeon said
as he stood at the foot of my high-tech bed.

My sternum is bound together with wire. I've seen
it on the X-ray. I'm new. I'm bionic. My clean

new valve drives the blood with a neat tick-tick.

OLIVER BERNARD

Engine Driver Poem

Here I am, dying to the world,
Which I've been doing all the time without
Giving it much thought, being more concerned
About tomorrow or next week.
                            'Next year
I'll do it differently' I used to say.
Life was just locomotion, rails and signals,
Points and crossings ahead. What terminus?
If like Jean Gabin in *La Bête Humaine*
I were to yell, go mad, give up, jump off,
There still would be no terminus but mine.
My fireman friend would know better than all
The officials, passengers, police what happened.
What happened on the inside? I'd forget.
The grain dies. Flesh forgets. All grass is grass.

JOE BIDDER

Sun and Stucco

Stuck between wind and sun
Between sun and stucco.

Lizards — there are none.
Birds — absent.

Here we are the meat.

Fuerteventura:
South of Cabo St Vincente
North of Dakar.

Fled from industry
We become its merchandise
Oiled and rotating
On this volcanic lava spit.

Fuerteventura — 'strong wind': one of the Canary Islands

White Knuckled

Three fingers of granite straddle the beach,
point at Turkey. Yesterday we sunbathed
on their flat smoothness then failed to reach
St. Hilarian by five: stopped by soldiers.

Today we drive through the Kyrenia Range,
search in vain for Buffavento but find
a volcanic crater sprawled across mountain,
valley and river. Blasted desolation.

We twist through razor-edged hills.
You grip tight to your seat, white knuckled,
vertigoed by the escarpment, silently
praying to a god you don't believe.

Remember that summer in Anatolia?
A narrow hair-pinned mountain track — wheels
spun on loose stones. You wanted to flee.
We heard they bombed Kurds fifty miles away.

Rainham Cemetery

Not a blade of grass,
not a single tree
no trace of a flower
to grace this barren place
where cheerless wet winds
whip from the desolate Thames.

A sea of rearing marble
fills the eye;
thousands upon thousands
of white-grey headstones,
bleak and cold,
send shivers up and down
my spine.
I tremble.
Maybe that is good.

My mother wipes dirt
from father's grave,
pulls a headscarf
over iron-grey hair
mumbles a prayer
in phonetic Hebrew.

She spent lavishly
on the black and white
double-sized
marble headstone
one half dedicated to father
the other half blank.

We come here twice a year;
she cleans the stone
with a wet hanky
mumbles the same prayer.
Maybe that is good.

Apple Blossom

When the apple blossom
fell across your shoulder
I noticed something new
as you brushed it aside,
tossing brownish hair
with a casual neck flick,
arranging your body.

Of course, your hair
was newly bobbed;
gone the long blonde tresses
that reached your buttocks.
Self-consciously,
you half-glanced
at passing men.

Strange how love must grow
and strange how love must change.
Now I must guard my memories
for time is ever on the move;
the space that lies between us
may forever distort perception.

Your opinions matter,
I shall listen closely,
or you will become a woman
too fast for me,
and I might lose a daughter.

PAUL BIRTILL

Last Meal

He had always enjoyed his food
so it was a hard decision what
to choose, and indeed he changed
his mind some twenty-five times —
keeping the prison chef up all night.
He finally went for a traditional
English breakfast which he threw up
on his way to the death chamber.

Wrong Set Up

I've been watching on TV
to kill and kill again.
But have decided I don't
have the right facilities
to become a serial killer —
not enough space for one thing,
and the walls are too thin — not
to mention nosey neighbours —
and I don't really fancy a career
move at my age.

The Race

Whenever the phone
rang in our house
my dad would make
a mad dash to get
there first — pushing
everyone aside and
shouting that he paid
the bill. He said it was
because he reacted to the
sound of a bell — but we all
knew he was a little unwell.

Counting For My Life

Sitting in my local pub
I find myself counting
the number of candles
on tables and imagine
they are the years I have
left to live. But seven
is not enough — so I stare
down at the floor and count
the number of discarded fag-ends —
though nine is still too short —
so I turn my attention to the spirit
bottles behind the bar and with some
relief count fourteen — that's more like it.

Watching The Box

It's not dying I so much mind
but everyone watching the box —
my box — staring, imagining —
recalling their own particular
moments with me, and me not being
able to communicate, rest or even
die with such a concentrated force
of eyes watching me. And at the burial
too — all eyes on me again — then the
wake — everyone talking about me and
in my flat — is there no peace?
No I'll have to wait until they spout
that famous cliché life goes on and
then forget about me.

SARA BOYES

Journey

I am going east
over the marshes and the road
in me is blacker than the night.
It is utterly black. There is not one glimmer
or chink of light
or slightly less than deep deep black.
It is a feeling within
this road over the marshes.

The other cars
going on the eastward journey —
and once over the other side
the small houses and shops — are delineations
which on the first occasion
I barely notice. And it is this
which I am now subscribing to:
my own body freely moving.

I stretch out
to touch the world towards the east,
or turn and touch my own house
back across the peopleless marshes.
I yearn for movement. And you are here.
Quietly and firmly you tell me — Now
you would like to see me.
Now you must do more work.
Now it is time to stop.

Black Flower

Now inside the new house
lies the image of death,

a brokenness composed of small bricks and dirt.
And down the thin black line of phone

she tries to tell him how he should
indulge his feelings, flow with the black of night.

The house pulses with the desire
to embrace and hold all pain and sorrow,

to let the broken bricks dissolve
and like a slow dark night, open into black petals.

Plant Of Love

At the centre of a day
spent walking around the park is this plant

with roots, with leaves,
but the flowers are yet in bud.

And this plant is not part of the day of life.
No! The moon eclipses and makes

the leaves a delicate grey and the roots also.
And it is in the darkness,

conversation turning partially on commonplaces,
that his eyes

catching her eyes
his hands flutter for her

and her mouth,
yearning, at the same moment

seeks to kiss his cheek.
All this can remain a negative

or can travel out
flowering.

ALAN BROWNJOHN

An Alteration

I saw a sea-change that came suddenly,
As they are not supposed to. In the three
Miles or so between Brancaster and where
The North Sea becomes the Wash, the large share
The saltmarsh takes of the landscape finishes
Slowly in dunes and reeds, diminishes
To mud and sand behind the rising banks
Which keep the ocean back. Beyond those, ranks
Of breakwaters split the waves, cargoes of rocks
Are held by wire meshes. Here the sea knocks
And goes away answered and forbidden, sent
Back to the hectares of its own element.
For stretches of this coast it stays like that,
A wind-wrought beach surviving, vast and flat,
Not sucked away by ravagements of tide.
But in one place a sour soil has defied
Water and grown things; a dark grass has spread
Where distant sea has left the beach for dead,
And samphire, rooting here in shifting mud,
Not in cliff-crevices (Shakespeare's kind), can bud
And flourish, threaded with salt but green,
A nominal reclamation. Except, where the sea has been,
It can return. And remember, you could find
Sea-change might not exclude a change of mind.

Found Object

An unused route back from the beach… But there,
A car, stopped; and a dog run over, where
The road curved…No — it was a teddy bear!
And we moaned with relief, having assumed
It was a dead, once living, animal, doomed
To die under the wheels of the fast car
Whose driver was hauling it onto the verge, not far
From where he had hit it.
                              It had lain splayed out,
With button eyes and open arms, without
Moving, abandoned in some child's small rage,
Throwing it from a car-window…Typical gauge,
We thought, of its value: Not a well-loved friend,
Just a dull chattel bought for it; not the end
Of a lifelong devotion, just of a brief phase
As an expensive novelty, a silly craze
Terminated in a moment.
                              That was what
We thought as we drew closer to the spot
And saw the creature lying on the verge
Where the motorist had placed it. One feels a surge
At times like this, of various inclinations:
Leave it exposed to the depredations
Of rain and wind?… Place a helpful card
In the nearest store window?…It was very hard
To decide what was best…If it was truly missed,
And grieved for, if it was hugged each night and kissed
Before its owner slept, they would return,
The whole pining family, search hard, and earn
Their reward in finding it safe and sound
On this grass verge of a lane, propped on a mound
Of overgrown earth in everybody's view,
So that it would be seen.
                              Then there came a new
Slant on the whole thing: what if it had been thrown
Quite deliberately? What if it could be shown
Its owner realised that its striking size
Ensured it would be seen by other eyes

Delighted to adopt it; thus, either way,
This toy would find its old/new home today.
And so on…We left it.
                            And, as we half-expected,
Within two hours the bear had been collected.

The Alcohol

The two modes: first the dull and logical
That belongs to morning; and then the second,
The desirable tinted mode of early evening,
Where you smile and you wonder, After all,
Was that penny-plain other one really so useful?
Or just a flat version of what has come later on,
A mode that grasps and simplifies whatever
It can touch? And whatever it can't counts as not
Worth touching anyway?
                            You can walk out on its ice
Forgetting its thinness, and even allow some tears
Of what's called generous emotion to drop
And turn into ice-sculptures. And then there is
A third mode, if or when the ice —

DAVID BRYANT

Impressions First And Last

The second time we met in that
mid-range chain pub in a
middle of the road lower middle class
seaside town I suspected
a noisy gear change was approaching,
whether up or down.
There you were trying hard to be
more beautiful still, red hair drawn
back like glitzy northern
club curtains revealing a
powder pale face, while your ears
jutted out in fleshier natural shades.
I wasn't sure I liked the image,
but I appreciated the effort.

I made no attempt to tell you
certain circumstances in my life,
and just spat out views as
accidentally swallowed Chinese proverbs,
skirting around the facts but
revealing psychological details
in the coughed up selection.
In the trivia department
we tried to read detail in
the popular culture we
both appreciated, rubbing knees
in the knowledge that Brookside
made us both cry once,
arms squeezed to shoot blood
closer to the heart when we
agreed that Harry Hill could indeed
be amusing.
The pupils in your grey eyes
filled reflecting images like
an empty television screen
promising more if you were turned on.

Tugging my forearm upwards
you shifted movements up a gear
and insisted amidst protest
we go back to mine.
We passed the rubbish sacks,
rubber cocoons swelling with
beans and fish on the pavement,
the odour of the alley waiting to
give birth on the street,
and followed the bloody footprints
to my door where a friend
of a friend drunkenly kicked his
foot through a car window
and in a limping sprint
spurted his life to us and
used our emergency only phone
to dial 999 whilst my flatmates,
high on ketamine,
dribbled obliviously in a better scene.

You spun on your heels.
You looked betrayed.
You said 'You never warned
me this is what you were about'.
Just understand that
until you claimed it,
until I saw the chaos with you,
I had no idea what I was either.

One Central Perfect Circle

He is stuck.
The slow journey home.
Frost on the line
or something.
Doesn't question it.
It's not anything
anyone has power over.

When he was young
he'd see tired underwear morose
clinging on to plastic vines
in tramp hair grass backyards
and ask mother who lived there.
Whose knickers were famous
every cheap-day?
He faces the silhouette
at one of the windows.

Her mouth 'o's as she
sucks on the wooden handle of
a brush,
the oil mounts on the canvas
like grease on skin
then flakes like dandruff.
It is someone
who is aired to the world.
Her expression is that
of the train with its
one perfectly circular
central headlamp
day dreaming its way
along the familiar track,
forgetting what it was made as,
and just doing.

The room is cold.
Frost on the window-pane or something.
She doesn't question it.
She looks outside on to the
stuck train on the track.
The passenger still looks through her.

PETER CAMPBELL

Night And Morning

The trains run down from Luton
Each hour throughout the night.
The clock of sanity lies winded on the floor.

Turn towards the thin partition,
Turn from the light.
The nurses' watch won't help you change this law.

The nurses read beside the passage door.
They read their stars and dream of nothing more.

The battered boys from Flanders
Rode this way from the docks.
They made them sweet and locked the passage door.

Turn towards the cold partition,
Turn away from their touch.
They've left those fields and joined a greater war.

Their names are scratched within the linen store.
The clothes you cadge are still the clothes they wore.

Men drove a railway eastward.
One spur beyond the halt.
It curved within, beyond the workyard door.

Turn away from the cold partition,
Turn towards their touch.
You have to wake, you have to face the dawn.

The pigeons land and strut upon the lawn.
They peck the bread the nursing staff have thrown.

The morning trains speak differently,
Their thunder tuned by sight.
The clock has changed its digits and its tone.

Turn from the thin partition,
Turn towards the light.
The floors are bright, the floorboards still unclean.

You lose the night, your ancestors are known.
Only the clock and you are in the wrong.

First World War casualties were sent to Napsbury Asylum, often disappearing into the mental health system.

JULIA CASTERTON

Stopping By Woods On A Snowy Evening In My Mind

Although I didn't know these woods as well as you
I knew them for a while. They were lovely, it's true
But I didn't love them. Why, I didn't know, then.

As the cattle and sheep farmers had moved west
To Oregon, perhaps, or California, the trees were more plentiful
Than when you stopped your little horse. More trees than people,

They said. But it was scrabbly second growth,
The tamarac and cherry that run wild, that the locals
Tear up as weeds. Often, I would stand in the woods

Looking at an old cellar-hole alive with goldenrod
Or at the fireflies sparkling by the tiger lilies
And think 'Why can I not love it here?'

You were buried half a mile away
And pilgrims came to the New England town
To see your grave. I watched the beaver

Build her lodge across the frozen creek.
She pushed bits of ice out of the way, patiently,
And ferried twigs and sticks in her mouth

To make a brave and lovely mound
Out on her little island. This was when
I thought that I was wrong, and that I should,

Or even could, learn to love these woods. But then
A man from Hygiene who came to lay a trap,
When I asked him why he had to kill the beaver,

Said 'It's a pest animal, like the Indians.'
The woods then looked so clean, in my mind,
Like the disinfected locked ward of a mental hospital

That already I was packing a few things, to return
To my city, with its feral cats and city foxes,
Its dirty streets and its blest confusion

At what is, and what is not, pollution.

Here Is The Room

Here is the room. It shines, it breathes its scent of night flowers
So as not to intrude on thought, or sleep, or conversation
With oneself. Much light, but filtered, perhaps through marble
Cut to inch-thin amber stillness. When dark's needed,
One can draw screens of stained glass, glass the colour of
Icelandic ice-floes, Galician green, or the slow mauve
Of autumn sunlight just before horizons slip away.

If words are longed for, all words, spoken or unspoken,
Are walking down the mind's wide corridors,
Informally, as friends who come and go
But don't live here. The host is silence, who's arranged the room
With such slow sweetness, there is really nothing more to say.

One lives here. Not I or you, but one for whom
Personality, attributes, and all desire and pain
Have simply dropped and fallen away, and disappeared,
Or become the scent of night flowers.

ALAN CHAMBERS

Drowned Rat

'We finally slid into harbour like two drowned rats.' Ship's Log.

Although it is what I wrote in the log
I have never seen a drowned rat.
I have seen a dead cat floating
in the canal, its body puffed out,
stiff hair serrated into spikes,
the eyes the colour of fish slabs.
'Poor bastard,' was all I could say.

This morning the rain fish-knived down,
sliding blunt edges through waterproofs,
cupping the flat water into
spiky obelisks for dead cats.
Soaked, I stared itchy eyed at buoys
that came and went through white-out rain.
'Poor bastard,' was all I could think.

I have some affection for cats
but that's not why cliché crept in.
I can make no excuse for its use,
or the lazy oath, 'poor bastard.'
But, well towelled down, out of the rain
though I have not seen a drowned rat,
I can imagine one drowning.

Never Having Seen The Nile

I have not seen that imagined river
heaving its waters down through Bible Lands
past the old monuments to the Pharaohs
    and the peasants' urgent fields.

It was pictures and maps in leather books
mixed up with The Holy Land and Dead Sea,
the plagues a damp smell like mouldy hassocks,
    slavery a child's game.

The silt hung in the river's muddy shawls
slowly spreads a soil to the desert's edge.
Scenes from the residue of others' minds
    grow at a similar pace

to build again a mortal imagery,
the seven lean kine, an overseer's whip,
the plundered treasury and barren grain
    in the Pharaoh's golden tomb.

But The High Dam intrudes. I imagine
its blessing, the controlled fertility,
bringing an abundance that overwhelms
    this thin strip of earth with life.

I know the antiquities are still there,
either beneath the brown water, or saved
on the steep cliff, their obsession with death
    refined in a museum,

while I conceive slaves rotting and famine.
Perhaps books are best, or picture postcards
or to stare back at the sealed glass cases,
    admire exquisite detail.

Any answers seek too large a question:
though I can't leave that river to go swelling
through an imagined world, ignore the death
    consequent on fertile mud.

Raking Over

You must forgive me, my dear,
for intruding into your space.
The moon, though clouded, is full
and they say snow is forecast.
I thought I must just look in
to see that you were all right.
You must not mind me fussing,
I will go soon into the night,
the sky has cleared, there is moonlight,
you must forgive my intrusion.

But I will not go back
into that fractious noise,
though there is warmth of a sort.
I am very sorry about this,
but it is all too much,
drowning out whatever it was
you might have been saying.

Snow across the moon
lights up a bent shape sifting
among the rubbish dumps.

It keeps a body busy
even if none too clean.
There is something to be said

for the joy of smashing glass,
stamping flat a cardboard box.
Smells of used coffee grounds

mingle with sweet decay,
a confused aroma hangs
on the freezing air.

Fastidious, I wipe my hands
on the back of my old coat,
then huddle into the dark night.

What is there to go back for,
fractured voices braying out
across mounds of old rubbish?

Is there something significant
about that rag and bone man
picking over his pallid dust heap,
his creaking cart on a moonlight flit
to another part of the city?
Turning the corner the street is lit
and the door is familiar.

You must not mind this intrusion.
I can bring little of value
that can justify being here;
I am worn down rather more,
my hands dirty, I fear I smell.
I need to see that you are well,
or as well as I could hope for.
I will go soon enough this time.
There should be more rubbish for me
to rake over under the moon.

RUTH CHRISTIE

In This City

Translated from the Turkish of Oktay Rifat

We wrote this labyrinth city,
finally we tore it up again into a crumpled heap.
That level place, that skyscraper, belongs to me.
The shadow of my sword strikes from mountain to plain,
razor and scissors fall from your hand
when my grey horse whinnies in your yard.
I'm a hero, a coward, I'm rich and poor.
In the evening I count my gold,
face down on the warm stones.

All this is mine: my people.
The hunter's shoulder carries an unerring gun,
the hand of another holds weights and scales,
and one, bewitched by the wind, dives down
to the venomous, upside-down stars in the water.
My eye is on the roses, white roses!
I stretch a rubber band to its limits,
and while the gilded clock ticks in your hall
I gently tighten a slack screw.

Over us pass Milky Ways
peaceful like a drawing in blue crayon,
blue, but in us there's fear and worry,
buttons and buttonholes, walls overgrown with moss,
barriers that divide my tiny villages!
Every day in this city a skylark dies
in a net meshed fine as a fishbasket,
the chickpeas stink, spaghetti turns sour, bread's like a stone!
Whatever is ours we dump it all in the sea.

'Sumer Is Icumen In'

Translated from the Turkish of Oktay Rifat

Shamed and despised, so pushed around
a part of us wilts, a part is battered and bruised,
we've emerged as though from an earthquake, from fire.
Somewhere there are boxes of tools,
a hammer, some screws, a few bent nails,
a messy tangle of rusty wire,
a ball of clutter surrounds the saw,
it doesn't even work when you pull it out!
You've been living in cellars, smothered in cobwebs,
with cracked chairs and stoves and boxes.
One day you open up. A one-legged
armless doll grins in your face,
a neighbour gave it to your daughter.
Humiliations, insults, pain
crowd into your soul like the yellow bugs
that swarm under lifted sacks.
A train speeds by. The whistle shrieks.
An eating-house comes into your head.
Suddenly you're climbing wooden stairs,
the washing waves on the line,
the yoghurt-seller swings along the street,
you're back in a time you love.
'Sumer is icumen in.'
Windows open wide, if you wipe the glass
it merges with air. Those are days
when the sun never sets, long and quiet,
made pure by thought.
A bird sings for you in the tree.
You go shopping, saunter,
and look at the boats and seagulls.
You feel good. What could be better than this!

JOHN E. CLARKE

The Dictionary

on the inside cover
of our concise oxford
you had crossed out
his name with a biro
making me realise
that some words
are forbidden

that omissions
fill the space
of questions

and later
when we tried to
fill the white boxes
of your thousandth
crossword
the pages gave me no answer
but gave you
close synonyms
skimming your tonguetip

you slowly filling
the white boxes
with blue

JOHN R. CLARKE

Weeping Future

In homage to Francis Bacon, artist and bon viveur

I walk out of an intolerant silence
And enter a forest stiff with noise
Somehow that deathless deity lives on in the heart
In restless ceaseless variety
As my eyes are dying in a profound agony
Of stones pulled from the messy plums
Of the earth
And I am ordered by an army
Of bloodtrees waving infamous arms
Alarmed to see mouths gaping with loose satisfaction
Beside the squelching suction of reptilian intrigue
Loaded with impounded failures
Banished to the desert in a mess of smouldering lies
Cast in dense infinite bronze
As one perfect fingernail flicks to the floor
To join the unruly exiles of positive purpose
Rendered by a swarm of desperate pieties.
Lives encased within the endlessly
Tolling perfumes of farewell.

Anonymous Rooms

Bareback riders on saucers of fire
Pulling apricot skirts higher and higher
Wheezing on a dull wind of expectancy
As a wall of mirrors dance playfully to attention
The eye is caught off guard as the shutter snaps
Moments you will recall a few weeks down the line
Or years after in the shelter of some other life.

Nothing captures that urgent tingle
Of forbidden flesh the frisson of delirious anticipation:
Bareback riders rolling on a sea of flame
Stuffing apricot smiles into mouths of desires.
Will you listen when a knowing voice asks:
'And what did you do all that time you were away?'
Will your guilty conscience come back to thump you?

Ash

Two pound coins
And two twenty pence pieces in change
Her hand cupped mine outstretched
Then firmly squeezed
Held overlong lovingly
That secret silent communication
Charged with meaning
Sent waves vibrating.
Those four coins dropped
Became a frozen moment
Fragile as eternity
Until she finally broke contact
The way a ship slips from harbour
Realising in flushed reality
That she had lingered too long.
Electricity.
'Ash' for Ashley pressed to her lapel
As I devoured those eyes of smoke-filled mystery.

JEFF CLOVES

toujours à bout de souffle

for Jean Seberg 1938-79

on the screen it looks so easy:
steal a car
— American with a gun under the dash —
get chased by motorcycle cops
shoot one down
take it on the lam *à Paris*
— so easy

once there
steal another car
— Cadillac Fleetwood with power hood —
hit a man for his wallet
rifle a girl's handbag
— while she sits half-clothed
oblivious —
then snare that preppy Yankee
selling newspapers on the boulevard
make it into her bed
make it into the headlines

so easy
— when you have *Le Look*
that trilby those shades
the right knot in your tie
tapered jacket silk socks
cigarettes lit one from another
so easy with jazz on the sound track
action in the bars
in telephone booths
on the street
smoky trumpets and smoky cafés

and what of that yankee girl?
— the haircut no longer dated
but so hip it hurts
the Herald Tribune t-shirt

tapered trews
ballet shoes
eyes and lips so *now*
second time around it's she
who takes the eye and ear
talking of her need 'to be free'
making out she's pregnant
— a could-be would-be
masquerading as a journalist
at the press conference
for the Important Writer With The Pork Pie Hat
who flirts with her then puts her down
shooting an existential line
she takes so seriously:
'am I free?' she wonders
'am I free?'

the Yankee actress who played the Yankee
was murdered in seventy nine
the film made her famous in France
the French actor who played the French gangster
went to Hollywood
the film made him famous in America
the man who directed the film
became famous everywhere
and forever

he still lives in France
bonne chance

on the beach

land ends
the cliffs fall down
occasional debris rains
on transistor salty towel
the unwary head
hot curve and flank

a sense of danger here
unearthing memories
of aberfan and distant volcanoes
bright plummeting climbers

the busy fish seem safe
but on the beach
us dreamers doped
on sun and sex
take risks
oblivious or heedless it's
all the same

MARGARETTA D'ARCY

Death Is Expected

To be told on the telephone
that his death is expected
and would one come and see her?

You see Margaretta I have been thinking.
One has to give everything
and nothing is left
in the old folks' home:

So come and see and take
what you want.
Charles is very weak
and we must be prepared.

Oh Romans
furniture and things
collected over years:
forgotten Romans.

Romans to be put in my home?
but there is no room.

SIMON DARRAGH

from *An Animal Alphabet*

The **Aardvark** said 'I should regret it if
they don't put me first.' (So competitive.)
His primitive ruse
was simply to use
two 'a's, then a third. (So repetitive.)

The Latin American **Llama**
is sometimes confused with the Lama.
Two 'L's for the beast,
one 'L' for the priest
in Tibet, who knows all about karma.

'Are we in the church or the zoo, Ma?'
'Hush, dear! You must learn to humour
such populist features
as "Blessing of Creatures".'
'But in the next pew, Ma — a **Puma**!'

If you see a **Rat** (*Rattus Norvegicus*)
try to catch it: don't let it evade you, 'cos
they always have fleases
with nasty diseases
many of which are contagicous.

Sheep live on cold hills. Though endowed
with thick wool, it gets shorn: they say 'How'd
you feel with no cardy?
Hill-top life's hardy,
far from the madding crowd.'

Zebras look nothing like llamas
(see above). If you show one to farmers
they'll say 'Why, of course
it's only a horse
wearing a pair of pyjamas.'

I'm After Leaving Monaghan

Your husband comes in, swings his leg over the arm of the chair.
He complains there is no food in the house.
Oh, you've made sure of tea-bags —
hundreds and hundreds of tea-bags, in a big green catering box —
sugar, milk in two-litre plastic jugs,
bread-butter-jam —
but no real food.
He seems to think you should have got some in.
I want to protest; he could surely do it himself.
After all, you are lying half-naked, half-in half-out of bed,
and hampered by me, lying half-on half-off the bed,
whereas he is up and fully dressed.
But it is not my place to come between man and wife.
So I say nothing. I let my eyelids fall closed.

Your left breast is crumpled under my arm, nipple half-hidden in a fold of flesh.
I want to release it, move my hand a little, make you more comfortable,
but I fear it might be taken, by you or by him, as a caress.

I think I hear your husband say 'And what's up with *him*?'
and am moved, nearly, to say 'It is not my place to come between man and wife.'
But I may have misheard, or he might not be addressing you.
After all, apart from us three, there are two other people in the room,
who just dropped in for tea.

I think I hear you whisper 'Help me!'
But I may be mistaken; you may be whispering something else,
or you might be addressing someone else, and my eyes are still shut,
and besides, it is not my place to come between man and wife.

My face nests in the soft spun gold
at the crown of your dear, dear head.
Everyone feels at a disadvantage.
It is a tricky situation.

ADELE DAVID

Pink

Palefaces on the Mediterranean,
men inside pocket handkerchiefs
knotted at the four compass points
of shimmering peaks: pink as in pinking
shears that mess up the voiles
too sheer to shear though a twill
will do: pink tulle for the tutu pink
as peony: pink hearts with valentines
for Barbara Cartland lovers
with monk-pink pates: dress a boy in pink
and he'll grow into a girl and not a garage:
you'll be in the pink if you're up there, out
on top with a pink purchase, Pink Fairy Book,
pink afternoon: and Pinkerton who did the dirty
on Butterfly who's so sweet-sweet, floral
as a gillyflower in Shakespeare's garden: pink-
eye, and the pink of perspiration after squash,
or being pinkish, impolitic in McCarthy's era,
or as now, politically incorrect
in a pink hunter's coat which is red.

Dear Ms Guided

I did not send you that press cutting
to restart our correspondence.
I do not wish to communicate.
My decree nisi is final and I am now free.
If you will not marry me I will not
revenge myself in print, though I am
willing to go to bed with you.

As to the monies owed by the third party
I strongly advise against chivvying. As for me
there is no question of Mammon, the state provides.
I hurt no one by being vegetarian.

Other ladies acknowledge my needs,
to these I give my critical attention.
They never complain about conditions.
On the contrary, scarcely a month goes by
without some satisfied customer sending me
fresh notes of congratulation.

No one has discriminated against me as you have.
Therefore, I close our correspondence,
and remain, as always, utterly without spleen,

Your One Time Admirer

SUSAN DE MUTH

The Horses

There were girls next door
and I called them the horses
they lived with their mother
I called them the horses
they were all horse-mad
they didn't have a father
they were all horse-mad and
when they weren't astride the real thing
we'd be racing round their garden
with straws in our mouths
pretending harnesses and
leaping over barricades and screaming
while their mother
lay on a rug in silk trousers
her fascinating nipples
like amber wine-gums
offered to the sun.

My mother
whose nipples the sun had never seen
would always be calling me in
ringing her bell from the window
my father staring
framed at her side
and frowning.

My father said she was mad
the horses' mother
he called her the mare
the mare was mad he said
and she lay on the grass
with her fascinating nipples
pressed into the sun
amber wine gums
without a man.

Without a man in the house
my father said
the girls would grow as wild as she.
I felt a stab of envy then
for the horses
racing late around the garden
in the dying light of the sun
through their long lush grass
and ours next door
a perfect carpet
their mother the mare
yawned into a soft silk
perfumed shirt
while I in the crisp smell of ironing
brushed my teeth.

Their mother erected
a concrete horse's head,
tossing wildly, mane flailing
jaws open, nostrils flared
above her garage gate.
It protruded from the red brick...
a tiny, wild grey head
with a colossal box body.
'The mare is mad!'
spat my father.

She applied for permission to build
a real stable
at the corner of her plot
at the point where our gardens met
and I dreamed of solemn horses
wandering through the trees
and brushing our fence
winnowing softly
and maybe they'd let me ride one...

My father put a stop to that
the horses he said
would bring vermin and flies
and the smell would spoil his roses.
He got up a petition and
I was forbidden to cross the enemy lines.

The horses moved away
the girls and their mother
and a proper family took over their house.
They cut the grass
they climbed up ladders
their father planted some shrubs
they removed the concrete horse's head
and invited us round for tea.
And my mother was always saying
'why don't you go round
and play next door?'

I took the proper family's girl
into their garden
and trotted over the carpet grass
I took out a rope
with a straw for her mouth
and tossed it over her head.
'Let's gallop!' I said
but she started to cry
she struggled free
and ran indoors
and slammed the door.

I sat on the grass at the bottom of their garden
and watched the solemn horses wandering
through the trees and long, lush grass,
winnowing softly and brushing
against our fence
I saw the shrieking shadows of the horses
leaping over barricades
and nobody watched from our windows
and no bell called me home
and I lay on the grass with my face to the sky
and offered myself to the sun.

BOB DEVEREUX

In Memory Of Paul Hancock 1953 – 2001, Composer

Cansford's a crematorium of sorts
For all those cattle cursed by Foot and Mouth,
A sullen landmark close by Bodmin Moor.

'It was the smell of burning flesh and hair,'
She said, as we drove past that quarry where
They burned the carcasses a month ago.

I had a vision of another fire,
Dense, stifling smoke, a burning chair.
A sleeper's cigarette had lit that pyre.

Singed sheets of music blew   The day was young.
About a garden.
A door wedged open   The morning sun still low
All the neighbours knew

       As I walked up the shadow

Paul was in there.

       Side of lanes to Jacobstow.

Man tries
To rescue dog   I saw a single magpie on the road,
And dies

       One bird for sorrow,

       And I mourned for Paul.

       Strange how the buried thought can be aroused

       To take its place beside the conscious one.

       I had not faced the drama of my dear friend's death

       Until I passed that quarry. Now it's done.

SITTING BULL: AUDEN: HEPWORTH & *me*

A boy of eight — idly turning pages
Propped up on pillows, convalescing,
Sandwiched between the mattress and a weight of books —
Chanced on the portrait of an Indian.

The subject was a chieftain in full feather,
The profile of an Eagle and an Eagle's gaze.
And then there was his skin: so tanned, like leather,
Crazed like the valley of some dried-up river.

The face slipped into this child's subconscious
And lodged itself amongst the folds of memory.
A face to conjure with.
It lives there to this day.

It was a map of Sitting Bull's existence,
An emblem of his wisdom and his age.
But it was more than that.
It had such dignity,

That dreamed-of face I coveted for me.

AUDEN
I was at art school when I saw his photograph.
My friend said, 'Do you know your Auden?
Have you read him?'

I hadn't read him but I knew that face.
That tracery of furrows ploughed so deep
It was a face I'd seen in sleep.
It was a dreamed-of face.

Oh so much life must slumber in a face like that.
Oh so much living fat and living lean.

It was a knowing face.
Not just a poet's face
                    Much more
                            A history.

THEN THERE WAS HEPWORTH
Have you seen her picture in the museum case
Downstairs, before you step into her garden?
Now there is a face.

Well, I saw that portrait or one much like it
In some catalogue, or in some exhibition

Not long before I moved down here from London.
I thought it was the best thing in the place.

Salt air, and marble dust, and squinting,
Screwing the eyes up,
Letting the tips of fingers do the work
And walking on the moors, out in all weathers
And pain, and too much drinking, and caring
And not taking care,
And smoking… I almost missed out smoking
And not caring enough about herself;

All this and more had made the map she wore
          But in that wrack of lines there is a knowing.
It is the same face.

          And then there's me

I'm sixty now.
I'm gazing in the mirror
The crows' feet are advancing
But I am not ready.

I've seen some lean years
But I have not had the fat.

I have not spent enough time looking at the sun.

Can I be eight again?
Oh please let it be simple.
Let me be dreaming of these marks.

I coveted a face but I'm not ready
No… it's not me yet… that dreamed-of face.

          HEPWORTH: AUDEN: SITTING BULL but not me.

BRIAN DOCHERTY

Cheers

He proffers the Seaview Brut Rosé.
It sounds like an Old People's Home,
has the colour of a Pensioners Special
hair rinse and probably tastes as if
it originated in the same factory.
I hate rosé, usually drink rioja red.
He obviously expects me to drink this
and be grateful he has remembered
my birthday again. What do you think?
Moments like this remind me I'm in
good shape but might be shanghaied
to a *Seaview* in the all-too-foreseeable
future. Nigel knows there's a Will,
knows to the nearest pound how much
this house & my possessions are worth.
He wants me to covenant the lot to him,
'Keep it out of the Council's clutches,
safe in the family.' As if I could pay
Nursing Home fees without selling up.
One day I offered to leave everything
to the Terrence Higgins Trust. Oh dear.
'But they're... but you're not...'
His splutter about queers & fairies
nearly had me phoning my solicitor
while he was still in my sitting-room,
looking so like his father I nearly
told him the truth about 'Aunt Betty'
but no, this narrow-minded provincial
apology for a son doesn't deserve
my history. I wish myself Good Health.

Pearls

Cause two sorts of envy. Roughly.
Urban poor who slide their arm
round you in public, finger your assets,
slip them off, then stroll around
to their local Cash Converters.

Or petty-bourgeois snobs who sneer
'cultured' as if they could tell,
knowing the strings they calibrate
could be from a Jacques Cousteau location
or simulated & matched convincingly.

Both ache to be tanned & titled,
their inheritance snug in a vault
or behind a Rembrandt in a safe
whose security gallops the CID round
without any *If it happens again.*

Ownership is oblivious to envy,
treats insurance as property tax,
expects the Uniforms to hand out
lessons in geography & manners
to anyone who forgets their place.

Ringed & pierced nieces make videos
profiling women pearldivers in Japan.
Wearers marry into Corporate culture,
trophy wives in TransNationals whose
byproducts pollute the pearls' habitat.

Their Family Trust owns the Jewellers
where cultured strings change hands.
Discretion is inscribed on AmEx slips.
Baroque and *farmed* are mere subtext here.
Who would be vulgar enough to ask?

Tales From The Saloon Bar part 242

I prefer restaurants with inspectable kitchens
either the sort offering traditional fare,
simple food with strong flavours quoting
an idea of what it was in a previous life
or the trendy ones touted in colour supplements.
Y'know why Chinese chefs always charge out
waving a chopper of Cantonese verbs
if you mistake the kitchen door for the loo?
They don't want you to check the microwave
behind the noodle vats where they prepare
cats & dogs captured before opening time,
the ping ping ping harmonised by the cashtill
ringing up the lunchtime dim sum orders.
Chop 'em into a bin then into the wok
to impersonate that day's Chef's Special.
All those Gerrard St. duck racks are glazed
with sauce strong enough to fire Wedgwood.
Ever wonder where all that duck comes from?
How many duck farms d'you think there are
cluttering up the agricultural districts?
What's the duck/chicken ratio in Sainsbury's?
How many cats d'you see running round Soho?
Or do you imagine they import it along with
kung fu slippers, heroin, and Taoist statues?
It's enough to make you turn vegetarian
till you remember the Industrial Revolution,
200 years of heavy metals marinading the soil,
root vegetables collect those ever so efficiently,
cook 'em in aluminium, you got mass Alzheimer's.
Now then... what was I... talking about...

BEATA DUNCAN

Crane Beach

After the service
we drove to the coast,
empty except for birds
and trees turning red.
You wanted to go back to the ocean
where we all come from.

Anna, your eldest,
carried the cardboard box,
she tipped and shook it
and in the end held it upside down.
Always quick to swim out to sea,
you lay in shallow water

like a mass of grey oats.
I wanted to know
where your lashes were,
the long lashes I used to envy...
We covered you with lobelia
from the rockwall you built

and pink gladioli with purple throats;
you would have thought the satin bows
a waste of money.
I bent down to touch you
and felt grit like crushed shells.
We could have taken a handful each

according to how much we loved you
or according to your will,
but stood without speaking
in the fading light.
Anna's small twins were shuffling sand
into the empty box.

We left in the darkness by a full moon.
I wondered if the tide
would sweep you out

or you'd stay on the beach
for strangers to tread on,
and when I'd see you again.

Crash

He stood beside a wooden bench,
shapeless pants loose on thin legs.
Matted curls hung in his face
and he was shaking.

I went up to the bottle bank,
sorted empties into green and clear
and listened to the crash
of breaking glass;

filled my bag with grapes and avocados
and wondered if I had the guts
to offer him a meal, a bath,
the spare room bed…

Coming downhill,
I saw him by the wall
between Café Casablanca
and the chemist.

Pale yellow liquid ran along
the flagstones,
made an island of his holdall
and flowed on.

I quickly walked past
tables on the pavement,
spoons in cream cakes,
bangles glinting in the sun.

If I Were An Octopus

I'd embrace you with one arm,
write a feminist novel,
wash out your socks,
paint blue shadow around my nose,
drop arsenic in her drink,
play you a lullaby
with the remaining two.

Problem Page

Virginia Woolf is not a penname,
the writer married a Woolf.
Use of a pseudonym is unlikely
to stop boy friend or sister
seeing themselves in your novel.

What a shame Prince Albert
melted on the Christmas tree
and great grandma cried!
Model him in marzipan next time,
it will not harm her gums.

Well done! You have completed
a Dutch landscape puzzle
the Queen found difficult.
Why not write to a lady-in-waiting
and offer to assist Her Majesty
fit the missing bits?

It is not the custom in this country
to ask for doggy bags at parties;
but you could help with the dishes
and sneak goodies into bag
or inner pocket.

Feel free to send me all your problems.

JANE DURAN

Coastal

I love your old age,
days when you repeat stories
and the screen door opens
into the parlour of your kitchen.
Your neighbours are without
salt or sugar, wanting to come in
in their tucked-in dresses,

their mops put by,
those tribal processions —
baldness of husbands, sons,
bearded mothers. Fish scaled
and left in the smokehouse,
the sea losing its haze.

They leave behind conversations,
silences, old rope for new.
Your stories tether back
to those first porches.
Who can sleep in the summer months
under such patchwork —
the heat of the past,
the lighthouse room?

The seals have grown old
here too, in the worn-out
quilts of the sea, gusts.
We breathe the same air.
Some nights they look in at us
from the galleries of their whiskers,
streaked with salt, with mating.

I know each moment —
stories that wash up,
coasts that take and take the light,
the first beaten-back mornings.

There Are Women

Women who let their hair go uncombed,
long, grey, who hold their hair
in their red hands, move in confusion.

Who could cook, or embroider.
Who border the shiver of a man all winter
with their spirit, breathing in the fog air.

Whose clothes are unkempt to this day.
And who move sideways inside their shoes.
Seem meant for love anyways.

Who stand still when the tide overcomes
their large bare feet. Who muddle their sex,
their struggle. Who come in close to him,

whose faces are so close there is nowhere to hide.
Women for whom I would take the combs
from my hair and weep openly, face to face.

ANTHONY EDKINS

Resistance

The days are slipping away too quickly:
'My rats' I call them affectionately,
Standing on the bridge of my sinking ship.

I do not consider them deserters:
Their retreat is a cautionary tale
A call to act on a contracting stage.

Will I heed them or, beguiled by splendid
Sunset, let my ship go down, in step with
The quotidianly deceptive sun?

Procrastination is a friendly thief
Saving us from the extra bitterness
Of effort wasted on final failure
And leaving guesses hanging in the air.

Sonnet Thirsting For Adventure

Sometimes the longing's disproportionate —
A desire to drink new territory,
Even quite absurd little tastebuds of land,
In the homestate, in foreign anchorage
Or at the opposite end of the earth;

No need to name names, it's geography
More than topography that is the game —
Or a vague geometry of feeling,
Rather than an awkward excavation
Of raw metal, or rough hewing of stone;

Somewhere to sink down after the day's work
Beside a fire that keeps the wolves at bay,
With waiter bearing assorted bottles
On a silver tray — that sort of story.

Map Reading

The contemplation of maps was one of Fourier's
favourite occupations — Walter Benjamin

Fourier followed the contours,
His hairy legs and hiker's boots
Treading terrain, stubby fingers
Exploring all roundabout routes.

Like traffic cops or aerial
Photographers, his eyes surveyed
River, tumulus and barrow,
The nuances of sun and shade,
Names from earlier romances,
Currents called after naturalists,
Islands he'd all but forgotten,
Capes of close shaves, their rocks, their mists...

Fourier's maps were metaphors,
Landscapes, horizons of the mind,
Mirrors or windows in the walls,
Models of what he hoped to find.

JANE ELDER

Old Man Reading

Based on a lithograph by Odilon Redon

An old man reading in a darkened room —
the light streams in through thick encircled panes
and falls upon the pages of his book
on his bald forehead and his thick white beard.
His fingers trace the words, his face is calm
as if he read what gives him peace of mind.
His eyes are dark and watchful — what surprises
can he be hoping for, now, at his age?
Before him on the table other books
and burnt out candles catch their share of light.
The room is bare, save for his throne-like chair
and massive table where he props his tome.
He could be a magician or a sage
or pious reader of religious wisdom.
Does that face hold a touch of mischief in it
or is it wholly given up to learning —
serious, serene and ageless? Does he read
the history of his life, hidden till now
when he can find the thread that makes the sense
to trace the path out of the tangled web
the sunbeams seem to weave in the dark room?
No clock ticks there, only his breathing stirs
the silence of the dusty atmosphere —
the regular turning of the page once read
all the event he hopes for, all excitement.
Still as an hourglass when the sands have settled
he waits and reads there in the darkened room
and still the light streams in, ever, for ever.

Landscapes

Based on the work of Peter Lanyon

1. MOVEMENT IN SPACE

The sky upon my back, I climb the hill.
The sea's behind, below me. Below thought
I feel their changes — light warmth air
their silent mode of telling — root in me.
This is my landscape, known by heart,
known in my guts. No need of learning
the space around me, or the space within.
I move in it, it moves in me.
Look, here I draw the line, white chalk on brown
to mark the undivided field.

2. CONSTRUCTION

My fingers find their way
                              they play
gather select arrange —
they do not think, they make. I do not know
what they are making nor what it will mean.
Glass, cardboard, metal,
paint, plastic, wood combine
to form a landscape known, but never seen.
My fingers take a walk there
                              see their path
which some day in the future I shall find.

3. IN FLIGHT

Scarlet for excitement, scarlet for danger
scarlet of bright arterial blood-jet
a dash a spurt on blues and greens
enlivens the sky, the sea, the ground
to speed this dream-race of my joy
race with myself race into silence
the arrow flies, does not come back.

Paintings Of The Camden Town Group

Theirs was a world which has only just disappeared.
It hung around my childhood — a dull plum colour
bruise-blue, wine-stain, purple-black damson jam
dried mustard, chocolate, varnished furniture brown. Variety of mud
with at times mud's iridescence.
Earth of the earth, the everydayness of life
except that abroad occasionally lit lemon sunlight
blazed orange noon, closed violet twilight.
And these colours gave a strangeness to, were the other side of
the British temperament and the English climate,
the dingy privet of parks, the close interiors
coal fires, coal smoke, the stinging pea-soup fogs,
dark sunlight kindling the milder pleasures
of suburban gardens, dim mirrors
reflecting gloomy nudes with blowsy breasts
slack-bellied weariness of the flesh
for randy Puritan grandfathers' lusts
counting the shame, resentful of the cost.

That time existed still, when I was a child.
People I knew were rooted in that past.
I met it in their homes, breathed in its air
which left its traces in my lungs and in my heart.
So that now, repelled by a chill wilderness of formica
a waste of peeling plastic, the litter of liberation
from the rock-solid stuffiness of mahogany and chenille —
I feel overwhelmed by momentary nostalgia
for the sooty baroque of the old theatre, gilt under grime
for the yellow brick terrace with its carpet-sized gardens
and could almost cry: O come back, yesterday
with all your faults. Everything is forgiven.

DAVID ELIOT

My Grandmother

My grandmother, every Friday night,
Would hold her hands to the Sabbath Candles, see
Wax stalks luminous as bone.
Outside, the vine of tabernacle night
Pressed in upon the window net
Like a fierce dark conviction.

Her strained, warm smile
Chivvied and welcomed,
Her head a rise of moon
Lightly dusted with grey.
Her eyes were tight with the Holy One.

Blessed be he.
She would rather die
Than eat on a Fast day.

Now my table's empty
But for a designer light.
The night hangs overhead
Tangled with impossible stratagems.

FLORENCE ELON

Expecting a Declaration of War

A storm tide drags the sea,
clouds drift into dark furrows.
We lie on the beach.
Your face, jagged as seal rocks
off the coast, slants
toward the Sunday news.

The rim of a Ferris wheel —
fringe of greens, reds, yellows
needled with steel —
arcs over the cove.

On the cliff edge
sharp, tiny, as through a lens:
boys march, waving
banners for peace or war.
Men on liberty
feed coins to telescopes,
point them out to sea.

They tick; click shut.
Our newspaper blows
over shoes, robes, hands, feet.
The speeding wheel above us
blurs to rainbow.

JANE FRASER ESSON

Four Spanish Widows

Tapping our white canes
We move along the pavement,
Eyes behind sunglasses.

Motorbikes roar past —
We see the dim shapes,
Feel the rush of air.

The noonday heat
Bears down upon us,
Scorching our clothes.

Four black figures —
Our white sticks try
To make sense of the road.

MARTINA EVANS

Manure

Maybe
it had something
to do with roses,
but somehow
I thought
that the word manure
meant sweet.
Tiptoeing across
the stiletto heel pocked floor,
I lifted my nose like a dog
to drink in draughts
of my sister's bedroom,
Atrixo, Pond's cold cream,
hairspray and Tweed
parfum de toilette spray.
Now, sea breeze incense,
strawberry lip balm
and toffee lipstick
all over your glitter spilled
pillow,
bring back those innocent days
when I would have told you
the same as I told my sister,
that your smell
is as nice as
manure.

HARRY EYRES

'I Want To Tell You'

I want to tell you
that it was all an act
if I seemed to be sailing through,
nonchalant, or with sang froid,
inside I was shitting bricks
for most of my so-called youth.
Nothing ever seemed certain,
the ground about to swallow me,
the air full of black rooks
like souls scared out of their wits;
and if you asked if it had to be so
what would I answer to that?
I could speak of Benjamin's angel
facing into the ruins of the past
and blown backwards into the future
or I could unhunch my shoulders,
turn slowly round,
and begin to breathe.

Catullus 83

When hubby's listening, Lesbia bad-mouths me,
which makes that gormless idiot grin with glee.
The mulish dunderhead! Can he not see
that if she seemed oblivious, or inured
against me, it might mean she was cured.
In fact her snarling insults indicate
she remembers and, much graver, she's irate.
She fumes, she burns, she speaks — good news for me!

Catullus 40

Crazed Ravidus, what's the kamikaze urge
that drives you straight into my iambics' sights?
Have you unwisely asked a god to help
entangle us in some ridiculous brawl?
Or is it just desire to figure in
a gossip sheet that's causing all this fuss?
Is being a celebrity all you care about?
You'll get your wish and pay a heavy price
for daring to set your cap where my heart's fixed.

Catullus 43

Greetings, hare-nose,
flat-foot, wall-eye;
stubby-fingered, slavering-mouthed,
sewer-tongued mistress
of the failed Formiae swindler.
Are you really considered
a beauty in Cisalpine Gaul?
Are you mentioned in the same breath
as Lesbia, *the* Lesbia?
What an age, what total
lack of discrimination!

The Light Of Postmodernism

River Thames, Butler's Wharf, June 2001

The moon is a question-mark
with the point of the question-mark missing.
A warm wind up from the estuary
ruffles the real-looking water
into real-looking brown-grey waves.
Everything here which was what it seemed,
a spice warehouse, a tug-boat,
everything which referred to a working
world, to specific smells,
is now just a groundless allusion:
Cardamom Towers, Cinnamon Towers,
condominia with their Japanese garden
and their balconies where a man has
his feet up on an iron chair
but with his elbow cocked
in mobile phone position
is not really looking
at the thin moon
or the disturbed water
or this place
where meaning has taken a lurch sideways.

SHELAH FLOREY

Came True

Almost fairy-tale,
an Arabian in a cave
points a long finger
towards the gold towers
of the West —
'People not my people
shall not live.'

But then he stretched
his hand to the sky
and cast his spell
till planes and passengers
on ordinary journeys
became weapons that
brought giant buildings down.
His enemies — busy there
in the morning — were changed
to the specks we saw
that fell a long way
through the air.

Streetwise

Video recorder, jackets,
a spade, books
in a cardboard box—
the people putting their
things into a van
are hot, can't wait
their thoughts already
on another place. They're
just borrowing this scene,
getting it over quickly,
fast-tracking to and fro
across a pavement

that now — this afternoon
and in the sun —
looks particularly serene
and do-nothing,
with all its years in tow.
Basking a bit —
it's not going, is it.

New Year 2000

My video clock
I'd been expecting great things of,
did not, as some experts had predicted,
mistake the century
and go back into the past,
still in the room with me,
start living in the days
of Sherlock Holmes,
gas lamps and carriages.

It knew at once it wasn't 1900,
ignoring all the talk
and with no pretence at charm,
even as I looked,
it zapped into the proper year
and stayed there.

This was my first indication
that nothing was going to go wrong.
The doom merchants had let us down.
No bug had got in,
no chaos in the morning,
no news of a crash at power stations
or glitch of any kind
sending world markets in a spin.

As was not unusual for the time of year,
old wars went on,
a painting was stolen from a museum.

DAVID FLOYD

Valentine's Day 2002

So, here we are again
I'm at home,
Reading a book on theology
You are somewhere else

You know,
I've never believed in love
Always seen it as a
Capitalist construct
To sell expensive cards
And chocolates
With unnecessary packaging

And here I am again
Just like last year
Waiting for you to prove me wrong

Class Joker

In maths
he eats four jam doughnuts.
We laugh

He cuts his finger
and scribbles in blood.
We discuss algebra

He jumps out of the window.

Everybody In

We'd seen it coming for a long time,
the day it became an imprisonable offence
not to be in prison.

There was a couple of million of them
that was the surprising thing,
how many survived to the end.

They'd survived the bans on drink,
drugs and extra-marital pillow-fighting,
rational thought, irrational thought
and coughing in a seditious manner.

Now they were being herded along by guards,
who had to be back inside by six o'clock.

There was no protest,
if they'd been that sort
they would've been inside already.

The next morning there was
a message over the radio
informing us that we knew the rules
and that anyone stepping out of line
would be chucked out.

War In The Playground

At school today
Ben punched Peter
in the mouth
for no reason
and knocked out
two of his teeth

Mrs Wilson was very angry
and told Ben
he was in big trouble

Ben said that
Peter was always
punching other people
and that his invisible friend
had told him to do it

Then he ran out of the school gate
and went home

So Peter went up to
some of Ben's friends
and started kicking them
for no reason

Mrs Wilson shook her head
and went to make a cup of coffee

NIGEL FOXELL

The Wright Brothers

Romantic they weren't:
single, teetotal,
on their run's eggs
they pencilled the laying date
and yes
ate them ordinally.
Tradewise
they made and mended bicycles.
They knew
the recalcitrance of machinery,
the intimate empathy
in tackling. So
while dreamers dreamed
they flew.

DNA

It's raining DNA.
On the canal bank
willows pump down
downy seed
till water whitens
with cotton-wool flecks floating,
and capsules of DNA,
ancestral info,
vital,
when fluff's no more —
no more than parachutes
jettisoned on landing.
And they
plus catkins, trunk, and Uncle-Tom-all
all aim, aim solely
at sowing banks,
data banks:
not any old data
but coded glyphs
marked willow.
It is raining DNA,
raining instructions,
raining algorithms.
This is no metaphor:
it's raining floppy discs.

LEAH FRITZ

On The One Hand

This could be taken as confession, almost.
I tend to qualify, where possible.
There! You see? If that's far from a boast,
it isn't quite what might be called a full
apology. Somewhere between the down-
right negative and clarion positive
(décor in shadowy tints of grey or brown,
perhaps), I find it comfortable to live.

It's an uncertain world, I think, although
the sun will rise and, in due course, we die.
But clouds may hide the sun, and who's to know
just when 'due course' has run its course? What I
most fear's the Absolute. You must admit
that's really very scary, isn't it?

What I Am Learning

What I am learning — oh, so much! Each day
new lines entangle webs like beaded curtains
twisting as you move. If I could paint,
thin meshes would obscure sheer films that float
benignly over human forms. Abstractions
fill a place too sensuous to call
a mind, demanding furtiveness. I see —
not quite: resisting definition with
a rabbit's wisdom, learning backwards
at terrific forward speed as light turns round
and waves of heat feverishly shiver.
This is release. Mostly I'm not afraid,
cool in the shade of concrete introspection,
bypassing reason, racing to perception.

The Persistence Of...What?

In common parlance, fashion is a whore,
a magpie in the dustbin of sensation
who uses art to rise above his station,
the gleaming surface promising much more
than any body possibly can give.

As at World's End a mirror-image clock
reverses time, so fashion takes its turns
in somersaults to praise the old and spurn
the new, and then rolls back again to mock
the old. After all, a person has to live.

And what is art, if not perpetual
surprise, a dalliance with beauty; truth?
Take fashion's arm. He'll lead you to fame's booth
at art's bazaar, teach you the rituals
that wind the heart and keep it fairly skipping

until the mind's reversal at world's end.
Do you remember when you wound a watch
every morning and it never stopped?
Now, when batteries run down, it's dead.
I wonder whether Dali's are still ticking.

Friends

for Irina Ratushinskaya

You say you bring your friends good luck, your own
a roller-coaster ride: gradual
ascent to first plateau, a jiggling hint
of sudden twists to follow — then straight down
to hell. Only, no up-again, it seemed.

The mechanism stuck. Then friends from near
you knew and friends from far away you didn't
sent the necessary oil, and off
you flew, your landing gradual and safe —
a borrowed miracle you would return.

You say your poems come from 'somewhere else.'
You write them in your head. As once in jail,
where, halfway through a poem, you were… freed!
(To be continued…when you got back home.)
Seamless, it reads, by way of illustration

'The mind intensifies in concentration
to stay alive,' I do not say — but breathe.
We hear each other breathe. 'I have a friend
who needs me now.' You pause, and kindly add:
'Please stay with us, if ever you're in Moscow.'

KATHERINE GALLAGHER

The GM Scientist

carries the storm
from one field to another

His genes glow
with intention

He has tremendous tears
glass tears

No mystery
is sure of him

His merchandise
flashes neon

The flying seed
cannot escape him

Whatever happens
he will dance on rain

His fingertips
trade desire

Bees damn him
into questions

His heart
pleads candles of fire

His breakaway kites
don't hike warnings

He is stuck in a
spiralling alphabet

Thinking Of My Mother On Her Anniversary

I search her face across a hemisphere,
embark on one more journey.

Will you come?

She's ready with the thermos,
wearing her brown gardening-shoes,
her glasses slipping forward on her nose.

Says she's been planting dahlias
to make a summer show,

a new display for the place
she calls her *Park.*

Over the cloudbank it's candescent,
close. I dare her to keep up

with me. She shuffles answers
to fit my questions. We float —

almost sisters
in the glide of it.

Gwen John Swims The Channel

September 3, 1939. Early evening
and the sea soughs, sways
— a sketchbook washing calm,
its ribs carrying the meticulous rainy births —
portraits from her many lives.

She has always loved the coastline,
come back to it, the waves' fringed grip —
daily swimming the Channel — testing herself
against its heave and push.
Ahead, Dover's scribbly-white cliffs,
and beyond, the hills of Tenby —
its beach's curve, her childhood's
patch of sand. She has tested this sea's glass

and painted herself into its mirror
like a cloud passing over. She has more
interiors to match and place, place and match
as again she gives herself to the water —
its moody mountains surging,
pacing her — the archetypal swimmer
planing darkness, with the coast
clearing and Paris-Meudon behind her.

DONALD GARDNER

Dancing with an Octopus

for Marlo Broekmans

Fantastic organizer,
genius networker,
arms
everywhere at once.

Beauty
and brains!

And that enduring sadness of
insatiable sea things.

How not to feel
love at first fright?
How not to fall for him?
If feeling is believing,
how not to be taken in?

And should you slip into the ocean
and should he slide all arms around you,
then let him lead your dance
across the ocean floor
in one long quickstep glide,
or follow him in deepest tango swoon
down avenues of seaweed fronds
— watch out, he may elide
your life in one cold amorous embrace
and lead you to his very private place
where nothing makes much difference any more.

And please don't dare
to look him in his mournful eye,
lest he bewitch you with his stare;
his sorrow is an endless maw
it would take more than you to fill.

And don't forget,
ask him politely when the music stops
(serenade of uncurling shrimps and hurtling crabs,
where flat things flap along
to sea-bass undertones)
                if he will kindly let you up,
unsquelch his squelchers just a mo:

'Excuse, Sir Octopus,
before I finally go down
to share with you the unthinkable delights
of your château where starfish wink
and sea anemones bejewel —
        such darling little blobs —
                that turquoise grotto, your peculiar home,
I have to go
                and get my scarf and shoulder-bag — you know,
my women's things —
can you imagine, dear,
I must have left them on those rocks up there
                where all is sunlight and translucent air,
so different from your milieu.'

And back on shore —
one shout flung like a pebble at all that green —
'Dear Octopus I had to go —
d'you think you'll manage on your own?
I hope you'll understand,
I'm not quite sure we'd be compatible.
I'm more a surface girl.'

    O polpo mio, adorato,
    sei stato così garbato.
    Ma non posso immaginare
    di vivere felice in fondo al mare.
    Altra scelta non ho io
    che dirti tristemente addio.

And shivering on the bright sand, thank your stars
you did not join his store of bones.

RAYMOND GEUSS

Invitation

Shall we go to the sand-pits?
Yes, let's go to the sand-pits.

Will the air be fresh and clear
    over the sand-pits?
Depending on the season, the time
    of day, and the weather
the air will be cool, sultry, or mild
    over the sand-pits.

Shall we whistle and get a drink
    at the sand-pits?
Whistling and drinking are *de rigueur*
    at the sand-pits.

Will there be a crowd
    at the sand-pits?
There is almost invariably a crowd
    at the sand-pits.

Shall we take our whips
    to the sand-pits?
In what tree have you parked
    your brain, imbecile?
Without whips what would be the point
    of the sand-pits?

O Felix Morbus!

Numquam poetor nisi si podager — Ennius

Only when the gout's got me
do I get poetic.

Family

spring morning shout: AAAhrgh!
unheard-of catastrophe
Who stole mum's wine-pot?

	s	
	i	
	l	
m	e	
i	n	s
d	c	i
d	e	b
a		l
y	i	i
s	n	n
u		g
n	e	s
	x	
t	e	v
h	r	i
r	c	s
u	i	i
	s	t
b	e	i
a		n
r	y	g
s	a	
	r	
	d	

worms? check. parsley? check.
two tabby cats? check. rice? where?
cook sighs and strokes nose.

limp cherry blossoms
two drunken grandmothers fight:
only *one* beer left.

ΣΟΦΙΑ

Father, Son, and Spirit all in one,
three times the oracle spoke:

'*Take a good look at yourself*'
The pug-nosed stonemason shuddered,
but kept on lounging around
the gym, flirting with the boys.

'*Not too insistently*'
How much, though, is 'enough'
and how does this limitation apply
to the first injunction?
Protected by the Macedonian
garrison, the dandy
began to write an *Ethics*.

'*Transvaluate all values*'
(probably not, as he had
originally taken it:
'*adulterate the coinage*';
a painful mistake that had been)
Dog had a quick wank in the αγορα
and went off to search for someone
who could teach him Avestan.

ΟΙΚΕΙΩΣΙΣ

Menippos to Zeno:

'*Your dog is your friend till his dying day.*
Your brother will almost always
stand by you, and you may have
a couple of close friends. Cousins,
too, can generally be relied on
(except in cases of inheritance).

Colleagues, neighbours, fellow-tribesmen
will often help, even when it is not
to their own evident advantage;
foreign allies, however, steer
by the winds of interest, so take care.
A politician is your friend
if you have a cord around his stones
and are pulling it taut.'

Ramadan In Athens, 1710

I

The goats like
elderly bandits
on the mountainside
above the silent *kham*
piously wag
their beards
breaking the fast
with impunity.

II

Men and their frantic,
wilful, lawless ways.
For as long, though,
as the Blue Mosque
stands in the City
Allah will spread his peace
even to this desolation.

JOHN GODFREY

Big Sur Café

Take it all in: notice the way
the road you came on moulds itself to each
coastal indentation, rises, falls, but holds
a breathless height above the beach.

Recall the description; recognise
the grey, weathered planks, the loop of stairs
climbing to the deck, the paintings and warm pine
in the café, the waving firs.

Out on the veranda, talk to
the girl travelling north, your co-incidence as frail
as the paper parasol in her drink; be certain
that you won't forget her smile.

Take it all in: while you sit
with your coffee, five thousand miles from home,
consider how you were targetted here,
like an arrow, in search of a name

found in a newspaper and reflect
on how easily an airline ticket and a map
can get you anywhere, located so precisely
despite distance. Then get up:

look out over low mist at the sky
stretching westwards; watch surf curl at the elision
of land into water — do you leave now, or later,
or simply delay decision?

Take it all in — and, before you set off, be aware
that, beyond the Pacific, further than you
have already come, the land resumes,
goes on. Take *that* in too.

The Permanent Way

Down here, things move more slowly than they did
The last time we came this way with steam
Tumbling, wheels hammering on rail-joints,
The dry flutter of wind snatching at open windows,
And sudden views — always too brief — cut off
By stabs of stonework or a rush of sloped grass,
Rolling as we passed. Once, when ten, I asked
The Driver of the 5.13 if he could go more slowly —
And he laughed and flew the three miles
Out to Fishponds in a dash that left us breathless.

Now, with the track gone, we walk cuttings
And embankments, beneath bridges, and notice how
A railway imprints its surroundings — sometimes subtly
In the sculpting of land, sometimes forcefully
With structures built to last: each individual
Blue brick, precisely placed in the curve of an arch,
Making the whole as solid as Victorians who
Were certain *this* was the future. We look out
Across rooftops that used to circle in formation
Or up at the bottoms of gardens, the ends of streets.

'That,' my father says, 'is the house where I was born.'
We take a photo, joke that it ought to have a plaque,
Then turn, and amble back, trying to define
What's new and what still correctly remembered.
Up on the road again, drowned by the blare of traffic,
We look over a parapet: along the bank tall grasses
Lean in unison, as if swept by the wake
Of something slipping past; not a slow freight,
Struggling and spitting sparks, but a long express,
Its lighted windows flickering in the night.

MIRIAM HALAHMY

Beyond The Courtyard

'If we lived in Baghdad
I would cast your sculptures in gold.'
Like the sun on bleached rooftops
where afternoon air shimmers, mirage high
calls of pigeon keepers circle, dive, regroup.

Eyes to the sky, breath tight in lungs,
you release your plum, your darling
rehearsed for weeks.
Beyond bird cages, where shadows gather
a maid fills water jars,
ice-cold by nightfall.
You will sleep with your brothers under stars
huge as the birds you train.

In your dreams the courtyard hums.
Women flow in and out,
constant as the river,
pile pita on benches,
hands steeped in flour,
shape *samboursaq* stuffed with walnuts,
closed with a thumb,
stuffed with dates, sealed with a key,
marked like a coded secret,

until the gate swings open, you are gone,
beyond desert river, flying across English skies, Canadian snow
to breakdance with children of the Apple.
On city streets rhythms rise to skyscrapers,
sculpt rich blue light, throw shadows onto wood floor
where you have come to rest, dance,
break the limit of standard space.

My Uncle

Curator of family knowledge
he researched, turned up on doorsteps of light year
distant cousins, not always welcomed in.
White haired elder, deferred to, served first
he blessed the wine on Shabbos
taught the kids to sprinkle salt on bread.

Sometimes tired of his moan
the convoluted drone of detail
I took a gap, did not phone for weeks
then missed him, table empty,
my mother's brother, her cadence
hinted in his voice.

We treasured scarce moments
humour like a sparkler here and gone
and tantalising visions
'My father made a cassock for the Pope
in Madame Tussaud's,'
this, weeks before he died.
My niece drinks it in
reminds us of names we scramble for.
I groom her to take over our baton.

Washing Apples

Like Mandela casting his vote, I smile
and peel Cape stickers from green apples,
reel back years of vigil, marches,
taking my small son to sign.

He knows now why I said
at street stalls, in supermarkets, not those, or those
why it was never just an apple.

DAVID HALLIWELL

Two extracts
from a stage play **'Tom In Pam And Pam In Tom'**

1.

TOM.	Yes she
PAM.	he was so gentle
TOM.	and affectionate.
PAM.	I'd really like
TOM.	to make amends.
PAM.	I'd like to apologise to Tom
TOM.	apologise to Pam.
PAM.	But there's nothing
TOM.	I can do about it.
PAM.	No.
TOM.	Nothing.
PAM.	He wouldn't listen to me.
TOM.	She wouldn't see me.
PAM.	I remember the last time I saw him.
TOM.	The last time I saw her.
PAM.	I'd run in
TOM.	stalked in
PAM.	from the
TOM.	garden
PAM.	and gone upstairs to pack.
TOM.	and poured myself a drink.
PAM.	And when I
TOM.	she came down
PAM.	he was sitting at
TOM.	she stopped by the table,
PAM.	in the soft grey light
TOM.	of the afternoon,
PAM.	and he put down his glass
TOM.	and she looked in her bag
PAM.	with a
TOM.	how can I describe it?

PAM.   A precise deposition
TOM.   a riffling flutter
PAM.   · of the hands
TOM.   of the fingers.
PAM.   Something so simple
TOM.   and ordinary
PAM.   I'd always
TOM.   taken for granted.
PAM.   Something I'd seen him
TOM.   her do a million times.
PAM.   And now I'll never see him
TOM.   her doing it again.
PAM.   It was the
TOM.   last thing
PAM.   I saw him
TOM.   her do
PAM.   before I
TOM.   she left the house
PAM.   for the last time
TOM.   the last time.
PAM.   I went through
TOM.   to the gate,
PAM.   that funny
TOM.   old gate,
PAM.   which has to be hiked up
TOM.   before it can be opened or closed,
PAM.   and I
TOM.   she walked down the track
PAM.   that dusty,
TOM.   yellow,
PAM.   rough and
TOM.   stony track
PAM.   called Crawborough,
TOM.   just one word, Crawborough
PAM.   and I looked back
TOM.   and watched her going
PAM.   and watched him.

TOM.	she getting smaller
PAM.	and smaller
TOM.	going down the track,
PAM.	standing by the gate.
TOM.	Yes, I watched her
PAM.	disappearing,
TOM.	dwindling,
PAM.	dwindling,
TOM.	until she
PAM.	I reached that point
TOM.	where the track curves away,
PAM.	and the house is lost from view,
TOM.	just before you get
PAM.	to little Egypt Cottage,
TOM.	and she
PAM.	he was lost from view
TOM.	and she vanished from my life
PAM.	and he vanished from my life
TOM.	forever.
PAM.	forever.

2.

PAM.	Oh love love love!
TOM.	Oh love love love!
PAM.	I can't live without you!
TOM.	I can't live without you!
PAM.	listen i want to marry you
TOM.	i want to marry you
PAM.	i'll marry you in shorthampton church
TOM.	i'll marry you in shorthampton church
PAM.	yes that wholesome
TOM.	little church
PAM.	near charlbury
TOM.	reached by a bridle path
PAM.	nestling in the hills
TOM.	and set amongst fields and flowers
PAM.	and it'll be may

TOM.   and there'll be blossom
PAM.   and inside the church
TOM.   in its simplicity
PAM.   its peace and silence
TOM.   we'll stand
PAM.   side by side
TOM.   hand in hand
PAM.   before the plain
TOM.   and pleasant altar
PAM.   with the window behind it
TOM.   looking out on green meadows
PAM.   and woods and brown earth
TOM.   a view which has been called
PAM.   the most lovely altar cloth
TOM.   in england
PAM.   and i'll say i do
TOM.   and i'll say i do
PAM.   and we will be married
TOM.   and we will be married
PAM.   deep
TOM.   deep
PAM.   in the
TOM.   country
PAM.   in that special
TOM.   special place
PAM.   with its old wall painting
TOM.   on the south splay
PAM.   of the squint
TOM.   although we can
PAM.   see it clearly
TOM.   depicting the infant jesus
PAM.   making birds out of clay
TOM.   and breathing life into them
PAM.   yes and i
TOM.   can imagine
PAM.   the painting come alive
TOM.   and leaving the wall

PAM.	and the figures
TOM.	the saviour
PAM.	and the clay birds
TOM.	beginning to move
PAM.	and becoming vital
TOM.	and vivid
PAM.	and you are the saviour
TOM.	and you are the saviour
PAM.	and i'm a clay bird
TOM.	and i'm a clay bird
PAM.	and you put my beak
TOM.	to your lips
PAM.	and you gently blow
TOM.	life into me
PAM.	and as you blow
TOM.	i grow
PAM.	yes i am
TOM.	the bird
PAM.	we are
TOM.	the bird
PAM.	and
TOM.	we grow
PAM.	and we
TOM.	flow
PAM.	and
TOM.	we fly
PAM.	and we
TOM.	soar
PAM.	into
TOM.	the future
PAM.	and our
TOM.	wings
PAM.	are
TOM.	our bonds
PAM.	and we are free
TOM.	we are free

LUCY HAMILTON

Disturbances

She said that a wind
    blows over
desert sand chiselling
    stripes, ridges
or wavy lines

the way that chemicals
    move like
fluids through tissue,
    fixing genetic
patterns,

instanced the stripes
    on zebras
and tigers — the spots
    on hyenas
and leopards — then

as twilight soaked
    into mountains
she told me about
    the big brown
blotches on her body,

how each long vacation
    she returned to
work on the kibbutz
    where the hot sun
erased them for a year,

and wondered if broken
    symmetries
were like promises,
    contracts
or legacies betrayed;

I didn't know — only
    that my own
surface composure
    was the twin
of disturbances within.

CHRISTOPHER HAMPTON

The Night Sky

You'll make no new discoveries tonight.
The moon's an absence: gone to China.
Look outside — there's nothing there to inspire
But black silence and the stabbing lights
Of a passing car that turn the walnut-tree
To shuttered negative under the Great Bear,
Now tilted up to advertise the Pegasus Square,
With Cygnus raised like a crucifix
Above the southern shadow of an unseen pear.
These are nothing new. The night-sky's clichés
Make no talking-points: you recognize
In this confusion only its familiar pattern,
Punctuating silence with unanswering light,
Which comes to haunt a thousand years too late,
And leaves us doubting whose this future is
We sense there sinking down beyond the hills
As stillness blackens and the sky takes charge.

February 2001

Take that twenty-year-old walnut tree
settled there beyond the kitchen window,
thrusting leafless branches to the sky.
It's a safer bet than poetry.
It lays no claims to permanence,
and like the face of the Tollund Man
knows nothing of the appeal it makes
to the future — time unravelling in slow
and leathered proof, where last year's fruit
dropped black stained casings in the grass,
and left no other trace but the nuts,
some two years old, still waiting to be cracked,
and like the Tollund Man intact —
though *he* sleeps on, brows knitted,
skin stained walnut-black by peat,
through centuries of troubled calm,
the dark of his undeciphered dream.

Bedfordshire Sunset

I listen for it, for the signals
that flicker at me from a secret world,
sounds quivering with life,
where there beyond the garden wall
the red brush flares and the sky
burns into the linear silences
of Bedfordshire. What is it
comes from the heart of that fire,
that sense of animal heat
in the depths of the sharpening black,
like voices out of the stillness
and the bronze — a distant music,
hands that beat and slap
from somewhere far beyond this place
that speak the common struggle,
linking this Bedfordshire
sunset to the colours and sounds
of an anguished continent? You hear it?

Hands that reach out cannot heal
nor words weighed out like bread
give hope to those who have no bread.

CARLTON HARDY

Counting Lamp-posts

I count the lamp-posts as I walk the pavements.
But not that one the dog is pissing on.
I count the next one —
and the next — both clean.

Not that one, though, where a drunk
has his arms around its neck
nor the next one — which is out —
smashed by a hooligan's stone.

I count the one on the corner
and wonder who it's waiting for.
Then cross, through scowling traffic,
to the opposite kerb and the lamp
shining there is glad I am safe.

So I count it twice — which is just as well,
for I avoid the next one
where someone has been sick —
perhaps that drunk back there.

I go on, still counting friendly lamps,
until I meet one with its eyes shut,
and I look away from the lovers leaning on it,
his hand exploring under her pullover,
their tongues tasting each other.

Tiring now, I head towards the last lamp,
which stands outside my house and winks
through the bedroom window as I dream
of the woman who is waiting for me
by a newly painted lamp-post.

Reaching For The Sun

Freed from their shackles,
the people danced in the streets;
their rags swaying in rhythm
from sun-up till sun-down
and on, under the night sky
hung with the brightest diamonds
God ever gave to the poor.
Now and then they stopped for refreshment
until their feet would rest no more
as the drums throbbed in their veins.

With the old world gone —
they'd sweat for their own
till their arms brought down the sun.
Their men were the masters now
and good bosses need no whips.

Sweet promises ring loudest,
but wear thin through the years
and when their leaders wore politicians'
suits and drove rich men's cars,
the poor people's feet were too tired to dance,
their arms weary of reaching for the sun;
and they longed for a new messiah.

MELISSA HARMAN

My Father's Hands

My father's hands were trembling
As he poured the wine this Christmas.
My hand felt poised to help him
As it never had before, through
All those years of daughterhood.
I read the tale those hands now told,
Of the only child nurtured upon
An outsized plaster pedestal
He strove his four score years to hold
In place. A small boy's anxious hands
That kept forgetting to retrieve
School books placed on tube train seats.
Proud sailor's hands, doing their bit
On convoys in the Russian seas
To man the guns, wave semaphore,
Salute their betters, serve their Crown.
A student sportsman's hands
Putting safely into touch
A very odd shaped English ball.
Those elegant hands my mother so admires
Sieved disappointment through their finger slits.
They weren't the type to boil an egg
Or change a plug, or hold his babies—
It really wasn't 'done'. They pushed a pen
In offices somewhere away from home,
Posed, one on chin, one holding pipe,
For photos of the fifties man,
Swung golf clubs on a Sunday,
Held playing cards in neat fans.
Now they make a cup of tea or do the washing up
And sometimes hold my mother's hand
While watching Coronation Street.
My father's hands were trembling
But I didn't reach to help him
The pedestal might crumble
But he wouldn't give it up.

Still Life

She hid her light under a bushel
When its heat became too much to bear,
Covered her beauty with shyness,
Put all the mirrors away,
Bundled her ego behind her,
Wrapped up her mind in a shawl.

She hoovered her hopes and ambitions
Along with a tangle of house dust
(Then went to the dustbin later
To retrieve what she could from the mess),
Placed her talents and skills on the mantel
And dusted them three times a week.

Till her light burnt a hole in the bushel,
And she couldn't extinguish the flame.
So she scooped up her polished adornments,
Blew the dust from the dreams that she'd saved,
Threw her shawl in the doorway behind her
And escaped without laying the blame.

JAMES HARVEY

Outside

But don't you wish you could travel?
I knew to travel meant everything to him,

and was glad he asked me when we were both abroad,
we spoke on common ground for a moment

in Perigord, the land of the troubadours.
It was her stories gave me the impetus to go there.

But when I said I was going to my parents in Suffolk,
and you said *On the coast,* I didn't answer:

the distance between my parents and the coast,
to explain to you from abroad, I couldn't find the words,

the distances between Gainsborough's portraits, Britten's music
and what lies beyond the sea, I couldn't encompass.

I needed time to adjust to this new map.

Georgio Morandi's City

for Edward

You made your city over and over,
sometimes with minarets, sometimes with chimneys,
by arranging bottles on a table

and didn't need to travel;

I couldn't travel that year

and found my cities in books,
believing their every word.

Kaleidoscope

While bright outside it is dim in here,
a cool green light shining through the roof of leaves,
all other colours held inside the tessera leaves,
with each plate in the sun,
the only light touching earth, battered and torn,
moving about in the wind.

With light outside moving away,
this becomes cold and white, as green
rejoins the light no longer detained,
everywhere becomes uniform,
the leaves fall, returning all they had built
to keep binding light to air.

The light returning, the ground shifts
with green shoots breaking through and out,
setting alight the air, making fragile
blue red and yellow corollas,
delivering and receiving pollen
to and from darting insects
with senses delighted in the fixed colours.

MARIA HEATH

Ophelia

I

He hung in the shadow —
Nailed.

Dressed in flowers,
She stood at the lakeside,
Shrouded in snow.

A lily fell from the window.

On the sill,
A flame stirred in still wind.

II

Running in circles,
Wider and wider circles,
Around the lake...
Surely the centre cannot hold?

Melting snow,
Green grass showing through the January episode...

The white room at the hospital tasting chemical.

Winter poppies hiding opium eyes,
Around the quiet campus.

Beachy Head

I shall go as far as the lighthouse and back
Beyond the clouds of sheep
Blundering over the cliffs.

The stealthy waves are rolling through the mists
Opening rabid mouths
Wide as ambulance doors.

Waiting among ruined cars,
Crushed metal carcasses sculpted to the shore,
I watch the sea.

The tides recede,
Like hairlines blowing back.
The beach is bare as a polished bone.

Moving inland — the poppies look like real flowers,
Sap stems in the chalk soil — a meadow blue butterfly
Making a cross in the dark eye.

At Rottingdean,
The silver haired ladies play croquet.
The sails of the windmill are a mute silhouette.

Blackberry juice drips on my hand —
Tiny stigmata cuts —
Tasting of salt.

Motherhood

You,
In my arms,
Drinking
    soft, sweet gulps
Sweet nectar —
Your limpet mouth —
Your kitten tongue.

In the studio,
Alizarin crimson paint on the palette,
A dark red dye,
Oozing from the tube,
A potion of poppy oil and turps.
On the canvas —
A still mark.

I wait for you to cry.
It is too quiet,
This painting.

I watch you breathe.

JOHN HEATH-STUBBS

An Oxford Tortoise

Relaxing, one hot summer afternoon
(Years ago it was, and one whom I loved
Was there as well, but he's no longer with us)
Upon the lawn of an Oxford college garden,
A tortoise we observed among the grasses —
One, or so I'm credibly informed,
That once had been a personal acquaintance
Of John Henry Newman — desultorily wandering
(Quite rapidly, for one of his chelonian kind).
His intent, it seemed, was just to eat the yellow buttercups
That grew profusely there. He did not care a jot or tittle
For the green blades or their wiry stems.
Buttercups have a pungent taste, as I recall
From childhood experiments, and they are slightly toxic.
There ought to be a meaning or a moral
Implicit in this story, though what it is I really cannot say —
It all depends what attitude the reader has to Newman.
Or else it's just a pointless joke I'm playing.

I am a Roman

I can't now recall his name, if indeed I knew it —
One would encounter him from time to time, in the Wheatsheaf
Or in similar venues, in forties or fifties days.
What he did for a living I do not know, but certainly
His knowledge of Roman history was extensive —
An incident he told of — how once in Italy
He saw a little girl, and she was playing
On top of a high wall. 'Be careful, little girl,' he said
'or you'll fall down.' 'O no, I won't fall down, signor,' she answered
'I am a Roman.'

Carême and the Marquis de Cussy

'As a good book needs no preface, so a good dinner can do without soup.'
This was the Marquis de Cussy's retort to Carême,
Who, you must know, was Talleyrand's cook
And organised the entire catering programme
For the Congress of Vienna. Carême on his deathbed
Besought the Marquis to abjure his heresy.
I hope they're reconciled now
In some gourmets' heaven beyond the Pot-Star, far from that inferno
Of mud and slush Dante assigned to the gluttons.

The Ibises

A Bald-faced Ibis, somewhat disoriented
At the time of his autumn migration,
Finished up not in West Africa, but on Blackpool Sands,
Standing there lonely and frustrated, hoping for a mate.
If this had happened in Victorian times
The Ibis doubtless had been shot
As a rarity and put in a glass case,
Stuffed, as a centrepiece
For an over-furnished drawing room —
Or else, his corpse
Would have been handed over to a taxonomist
To count the bones in his palate,
The muscles in his thigh —
Cousin of the curlew or sibling of the stork.
But now he's been placed in a wildlife park,
Caged in a nice clean pool,
With plenty of food,
And surrounded by mirrors, images of himself
So he'll suppose he's among friends now
And a mate may come —
We treat poets in much the same fashion.

To find the Sacred Ibis now you'd have to go
Beyond Upper Egypt, to the Sudan or Ethiopia —
For he is Hermes Trismegistus, Thoth,
Grand secretary of the whole tribe of immortal gods,
Inventor of the hieroglyphic script,
Master of all wisdom.

The Glossy Ibis, on the other hand —
Purplish-black in hue, is, we are told,
A not infrequent visitor to Norfolk
And eastern counties generally,
But not to Liverpool or Lancashire,
Though some maintain
The Glossy Ibis was the Liver-bird.

In medio tutissimus ibis — 'you will go safest by the middle way',
The motto of all good British ornithologists,
The Roman poet's counsel to each one of us
Who seeks to sail among the clashing rocks
Of this agreement and controversy.

JOHN HEGLEY

The Party Spirito

Italy, Summer 2001

A lovely hilltop village party
above the seaside of Sestri Levante:
beer, chianti,
aubergine, spaghetti
and pesto on bread like chapatti.
The band play the cha cha
and what sounds to me like Italian village party music.
They play it well.
The party-goers swell
to maybe six-hundred.
The time is after ten,
now we leave, to spread the small children
in their bedtime.
Hermione, age three,
is seemingly not yet satisfied.
'What about the candles?'
It is a party, after all!
Approaching the cars
she says she wants to blow them out.
She is referring to the stars.

My Sweetest Blancmange

He always prefers to have something blancmange
whenever he has a dessert,
he gets what he can in his tummy,
he tries to get none on his shirt.
If there's ever blancmange as an option,
blancmange is the option he'll take,
there have been occasions when money's changed hands
to encourage the kitchen to make
something blancmange.
Someone asked him one day
in a casual way
what made blancmange so top notch:

the gobbling…or was it the wobbling, they wondered
which stirred something down in the crotch?
He answered, 'it may seem absurd
but the thing that I love
is the word *blancmange*,
it's French
and it's funny as well,
to me it's enchanting,
as you can see, I am under
its wonderful spell.
It's the pet name I gave to the love of my life
who has splintered my heart
like a fist might
a freshly blown eggshell'.

CICELY HERBERT

In Our Gardens — for Helen

It was almost dark and the air still,
heavy with honeysuckle and the day's heat,
as if it was always like this,
and you must have felt then how it will
go on without you, women at ease
in gardens they've made beautiful.

And I glanced up and saw you at the window
for an instant taking your place
to look out at women who will follow us
who'll sit at dusk as I sat then
drink wine, find dusty peace
in gardens after we've gone.

Tynemouth 1957

When I look back over those years
and remember that season by the seaside
that tatty rep, where I was the only
existentialist assistant stage manager
in the north east of England

when I remember how I lived on nothing but air, the throb
of my pulse, when I think about the way
the moon at night printed a path
across the sea, leading us on

when I remember the pub
on the rocks, lit by lamps
how we went down at closing time
to the chill, damp sands
slithered and slid
on the blurred edge of land
how the stars glinted far off
as we exchanged gulps
of brandy, mouth to mouth,
and there was no boundary
how I wanted to be with him forever

when I remember how my landlady
locked me out, so that I had to sleep
standing upright in a telephone box
that stank of brown ale and piss
when I think about how at dawn
I wiped frost from the glass
and watched the mist melted by sun
as it floated up from the harbour wall

and I knew it was going to happen
if not tonight, then the next night
now nothing could stop us
nothing

when I look back at all these things
I say to myself 'Is it possible
to have forgotten all this?
Was that really us?'

And you know it was
it was.

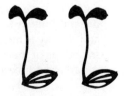

DANIELLE HOPE

Legends And Dustbins

Open the window Marcus
let in the night breeze to quell
the fires of legends that burn
from your low voices. Apollo above
Cerberus below, the whole class of you
evening silhouettes at your oak table
in this oak panelled room. Port passes
to the left. From leather books
murmurs rise — Phaethon the son
Hercules, Venus, Proserpina raped
the air heavy as Bacchus' wine.
Whatever folly you plot he will perform it.

Open the window Marcus
see those who scratch at hard earth
for fragments of history.
No soil to stick to the wrist as you dig.
No scheme of how it might have been
granite fort tops, mint grown
on the lower walls
tangerine cobbles that lead to a well.
No disappointment to spear your back
or to toss back to earth. *Your family tree
hangs on the walls of this room.*

Open the window Marcus
or have you learned ways to lock it closed?
At the corner of your meticulous garden
a woman searches dustbins
for scraps, she pulls at a newspaper
sucks dregs from a brandy bottle.
The grass sheds its colour
daffodils have turned their shoulders
distant thunder hums like gunfire
and the sky is hung with burnt out stars
fragments of methane and sulphur.
A barbarian breeze snakes over your arms.

Headlines

In California, the news is
Power Cuts Every Day.
There are too many air
conditioning and ice-making
machines. They de-regulated power —
my North Carolina friend laughs.
It didn't work. Contentedly
she sucks a fresh strawberry ice
clicks the automatic lock
of her long white Chevrolet.
But it's near crisis:
petrol will double in price.

Eric at the Movies

Eric is telling me about
the latest film at the National.
The Italian resistance. In the end
the priest dies. Painfully.
It is hopeless. Truthful.
And I am angry.
Why are my hands so soft?
Perfume sleeps on my wrist.
Rolls thicken my shoulders
my waist lolls like washing strung
out on a wax dawn.

Outside the taxis are all tangled up
raincoats stand on street corners
or flood from the dimly lit
tube station of Kentish Town.
I imagine walking the streets, watched
and watching, jumping at the tick
of a clock or a certain look.
In torture, it is a luxury to faint.
'The gentleman has sat so long

on the fence, that the rust
has entered his soul' misquotes Eric.

When even parking-tickets wound, how
could I have stood against the slow
stripping of hunger. Or pain.
Or stared into the eye of a gun.
Offering no more than to run
like the physicists
who made the bomb
to greet the enemy
that would have killed them.

Rhino on the 9.15 to Watford

I am a poem and I dislike Actors
lurching towards me with their sonorous

vowels and articulated consonants —
a late train jerking into a siding

wheels squeal, shriek, tut
as it stops, with hoot, shunt, halt.

The rhythm of carriages
bounce over connections

thunderous thuds on the points.
And all that projection. A rhino

on board, paces its cage, hoofs
clump on wooden floors, one horn

rattles iron bars, waving
a tormented gesture from Henry V.

A carefully guided missile
missing its target.

SUE HUBBARD

Sheen

Two suns shimmer on the lake like gilded lily pads
so it is impossible to tell what is lake, sun
or simply gorgeous reflection as the black water
mirrors the aqueous coronae back into the darkening blue.

Everything is still, silent, frozen,
as two dragonflies, like small helicopters,
dart across the surface in a momentary eclipse,
shadow puppets silhouetted against the growing dark.

Even the trees seem to be reaching backwards
into the water, their trunks refracted
between lake and sky into a thousand possibilities.
It would be sublime —

the firefly loch, the stillness, our quiet breathing —
if we could be confident of such a word
in this fractured, unmitigated world.
But you insist, amid all this improbable

loveliness, that what we are looking at
is simply water, that the sun is only the sun,
as if to warn me that this moment can be no more
than itself, must not seep like a stain beyond its edge —

and that like the reeds, the pines,
the mezzotint of sunlight,
we are only matter — simply a man and a woman
standing in the opaline dusk, and I acquiesce;

though what I really want to say is:
stop, this is special...
here in the twilight, standing side by side,
as two suns blaze on the surface of a lake.

Toad

It seems to come from somewhere
peripheral so that at first,
as it hops into my field of vision
on the sandy path, I simply think
it is the long grass swaying
among the arsenic shadows
as the darkness winds solitary
and indifferent back into itself
and I bend down on the edge
of the tangled weeds,
the dead leaves, the roots
and hairy ferns and am stopped
by something primordial,
frozen, reptilian: a yellowish
body, bloated, marbled
with black veins like Victorian
end-papers, noduled leather skin
ballooning with fragile breath.
Around me the night wears
a long face and in the hidden houses
sleepers exhale their sulphurous
sighs into the thick night air
and I know that with one step
I could crush him, this fat toad.
But alone in this unkind dark,
I am grateful for this small thing
breathing, just quietly breathing.

The Sower

Jean-Francois Millet 1850

Thighs braced against the curve
of field, puddled armpits
rancid in the freezing wind
he strides

diagonally down the slope
beneath a weight of sky.
From behind the ridge
the low sun catches

his left cheek, his hand, waist
the hinge of his aching knee,
the linen-gaitered feet turning
to hooves of mud.

An outstretched arm swings
then dips and dips again into
the coarse grain sack slung
across his hunched shoulder

where the halter rasps the nape
of his raw neck. Big beetroot hands
scatter seed on stony ground,
their moons all ragged and black.

A mercury sky. And his
scissoring bulk fills the frame
forming a large cross with the axis
of oxen dragging their heavy harrow

into the lavender, the rose-flushed dusk,
up at the picture's edge.
Beneath his slouched felt hat
his shrouded face foretells

approaching winter,
the brooding dark. Exhaustion,
waste. Memory of famine runs
atavistic through his veins.

In a ditch a hare pricks
its ears to the wind. A black
scribble of crows writes
hunger across the sky.

CAROL HUGHES

The Dance

Why do I sit so still and ponder the sweep of the broom,
            The lift of a lid?
A particle;
                I blow
                I twist
                I sit still.

Lead Belly Joan pulls me to dance that strange step;
                One step forward
                One step back.

The sky darkened...streaks of green and red;
My dance in blue shivered on the edge
        of those wastes from an exploding sun.
....
With the sharp boom of arctic ice cracking
        I took my
                    One step forward
                    One step back.

Diddle the fiddle.

That tune...and my baby with eyes dazed from
        the darkness and boom of amniotic fluid...

                    One step back to the sea.

MIROSLAV JANCIC

His Biobibliography

The poet swore not to write anymore — let History
Repeat itself foolishly — but alas, soon was asked
To submit a new piece to *Hearing Eye Anthology*;
He can only explain why he's stopped writing.

At the same time a recap could be done to check
If his belles-lettres have made any sense and impact
Which could amount to a self-necrology, though
As in his novel *The Prodigal Son*; we'll see.

In any case he shouldn't complain much nor accuse
Anybody in particular — he himself had a good run
For his money — it was the bad luck of his country
That compelled him to intrude on serious literature.

*

Even in his farewell *Singing Through The Town* when
The Devil comes to collect his due, the poet worries
More about the maladies of his beloved homeland
Than his own cancer; only he'll recover for a while.

The fact that he always manages to escape the horrors
Prophesied in his books and that he's actually outlived
His entire opus, diminishes his literary image, he
Knows and admits it in his African novel *Juju*.

It all began in the middle of the sixties when as
An ethno-mix he confronted the rising Nationalism
By the tragedy *Bosnian Plague*; he was naïve
He thought the freak could be tamed by kind words.

Comedies were futile also: in *Supper-Supper Market*
The Lady Bosnia withholds the name of her daughter's
Father; is it a Serb, Croat or Muslim patron remains
A secret both on the stage and real life outside.

The satire *How I Betrayed The National Cause* was a hit
But failed to bring to reason the jingoistic poets
He targeted; he only learned one should never argue
With national-idiots — they are destined to win.

Pro tem. he had to disguise as a libretto writer and use
An old heretic legend about the angel rebel *Satan*
Who unhappy in Paradise dances away to create his own
Separate cosmos and many a Satan's spitting image.

*

Reality's getting the upper hand over imagination and
During Hurricane John in the plane over Florida
An American female tanatologist scared to death asks
The Yu author how does he terminate his characters.

He goes numb recalling that they commit suicide
Mostly; at the same moment he finally realises that
He isn't always aware of what he writes exactly and
That sometimes he might be auguring his own end.

His *Bosnian-King* performs hara-kiri just to show
The question whose God should rule Bosnia is fatal:
His rebel Bogumil Tvrtko chased by the Crusaders
Charges against a new menace called Genghis Khan.

In a novel about modern times the fascist priests
Forcibly convert Orthodox children to Catholicism;
One of the victims, the boy named *Lightning Bug*
Hides in the belfry and takes off into the night.

*

As the nationalist madness eclipses the Balkans
He leaves writing behind, enters politics, in order
To propose *Universal Declaration Of National Rights
And National Decalogue*, but it's too late.

Spent at home Don Quixote was then sent abroad;
From the Equator *The Last Ambassador*'s watching
How his country vanishes in the blood of European
Tribal wars and apartheid he tried to hinder.

Adamant to tie the collective with his personal fate
As a stowaway he returns to his native Sarajevo to
Act and write *Spokesman for Hell* defiantly; yet
As a notorious anti-nationalist he wasn't welcome.

The hoary prose writer thus surrenders to the Queen
And turns to poetry — what else to do whilst drifting
Between exile, asylum and homeland; *The Flying Bosnian*
Are poems of a lost cause and a crossroad without roads.

*

Now he contemplates, fancies and writes in English
That has become the second language in Bosnia too
But his heart goes on beating the (former) Yugoslav way;
See the mini-play about maxi-issues *The Dog Walker*.

Asked if he's found peace of mind in London
What with politeness and gratitude he says yes, but no,
No one can possibly be calm if his homeland's been
Disfigured and the demons which haunt him triumph.

Unable to produce any consolatory line he therefore
Quits writing, hopeful that there are some optimists left
That he's wrong in the end as he wasn't at the beginning
So that all he has scribbled doesn't matter anymore.

ROLAND JOHN

History

To start with air pure and the streams undammed
a landscape still to be parcelled and broken by walls,
not yet the time of high halls, old men
and warriors' calls in the fields of battle.

But the beginning of terror, of loneliness, the panic
before darkness, victims of rocks, the Great Tree
rustling, the terrible sounds from the sea, black spells,
cantrips for victory in the caves of the hunters.

Later spears and the bleached, ground bones on the shore
Troy fallen and the beaked ships scattered
over ocean, landless men battered, proud captains lost,
it mattered little, innocence over, history's begun.

The clan time, family feuds, dynasties rise,
kings laid low, politics and intrigue, the upward
curve to the electric future, where bored with satiety
men in high halls hoard the relics of Troy's last kings.

Now time of gombeen men, bankers, jobbers and freaks
sure tricksters all and still brassy with power
but without a hero's pain, a dour crew of showmen
who would still cower before any god you care to name.

Just Visiting This Time

The expected smells, pale walls,
sharp lights, odours hitched to decay,
a background noise, the quiet earnestness
of nurses, doctors, their ancillaries.

Clutching books and fruit I pass
the easy faces searching for your bed;
they've moved you to a single room
and I suspect the worst.

Even in here the air emits
a specific wavelength of pain,
that anguish to which we all move
daily with improved proficiency.

Dear friend, to find you here again,
your gaunt face sharpened into bone;
through the drugs you flash that smile,
even your hair looks thin.

We talk such idle chatter, gossip,
I pass on the routine news.
It seems to please, relaxed
you recover some of your élan

almost your old self at times,
as we recall familiar jokes, shared
views, before discussing plans
about what to do when you leave.

Outside once more I know that
one day soon, I'll come armed
with gifts to visit once again
to find your shadow on an empty bed.

Weekend

So that was the way it was;
idling, pretending the garden needed my touch
nothing strenuous
on one of those days you can scarce believe,
the sun all day.

The country or the beach
you queried dressing in front of the window;
is that what you meant
an outing or sending those other signals
on a lazy day?

Down to me again
but better than shopping, staying home,
either way I'm driving:
how far is the sea anyway, which beach?
The whole day?

Not in that skirt;
stockings! Jeans and a warmer top surely:
let's be sensible
those shoes would be impossible
for such a day.

They make you tall,
yes, you are right and how those stockings
shape your legs,
of course I'm coming, don't smile like that;
make my day.

Fish Market — at Nice

Heaving catchments, live mounds to slice alive,
fins, tails, cleavers divide: no sound as
guts slop into buckets with the gawping heads.
Blood red as ours dazzles the cobbles,
eyes glaze, pale scales trace the wavelengths
of pain, their long agony of air almost completed.

So much flesh and death and always one stall
with some great tuna or sword-fish, the head
sawn off and slashed, the gills pulled out
and slit into a comic mask. The sluices run
with water and with blood, the eddying pain
flows back towards the green accepting sea.

It is the great fish that grip and burn;
the silvery slivers shoal, glide back into
each other, as if diving for safe water.
Only the surface haunts with gulping mouths,
unlidded eyes blinded in the staring sun,
no sound: the air vibrates with screams.

JENNIFER JOHNSON

Redundancy

I watch them chatter like children
with no sense of time
as if they'd never aged.

The women dye their hair to conceal
the greyness of their lives:
trying to forget marriages long-ago broken,
their wrinkles caused by sleepless nights
trying to keep families happy.

They try to look like the teenagers
who walked into these offices
some forty years before.
They flirt gracelessly: giggling
with the younger men
who submit to their expansiveness
red-faced with embarrassment.

Next month the company will close.
There will be no-one
to wear make-up for,
too much time to watch TV.

Will their minds wander
through a lifetime of regrets
as increasing aches and pains make
guilty secrets more unbearable?

Will they endure two decades
of solitary confinement
before they ring 999
to be rushed to the A&E
where, surrounded by nurses
speaking in soft voices,
they long to die, looked after?

Siblings

My brother slept for years under hedgerows
that caught his clothes. He says
he was lucky on his twenty first
because he found in the mud
a packet of fags — unopened.

And yet he told a woman how
he remembered picnics, country walks,
our mother's genteel talk and jasmine tea,
our childhood in Africa
with servants and morning glory.

I've told everyone how we were abused.
I must have forgotten the gold
woven in the cloth we wore then.
Only the scars remain.

Now I can remember, without feeling sick,
the music my father played.
With more holes uncovered,
I can play higher notes now
but still feel rage at years wasted by terror.
My voice stays young but
my hair is going white.

It's been a long time since
my brother signed me in where
oblivion is cheap. Even as snooker captain
he can't stop the black ball going down
too often and the mornings after
when his wife will exclaim
how she must stop walking into things.

Injections Of Oblivion

When they first met, her senses reached out
for new sights, new perfumes, his melodious voice.

Later, she began to feel dirtied by him; his semen
seeping from her, staining the bed they shared.

Numbed, she let him do it, pretended it wasn't real
like finding wads of notes hidden in odd places;

cash, she'd been told, he'd extracted
from those desperate to inject oblivion.

Later, whenever she met anyone
she turned away, preserved her silent tongue.

JEANETTE JU-PIERRE

Last Words

When death came,
you thought you could escape
its last breath,
somehow relive one minute of a
scintillating life,
cheat death by catnaps,
be a survivor of sorts or
capture experience in a giant hourglass;

Instead,
lying in state,
we watched as you gripped handfuls
of embroidered silk,
anticipating sulkiness.

Your rigid body baffled the doctors,
when we noticed your left manicured hand
sticking out of the coffin — pleading.

When they laid you to rest one summer,
your sunken eyes were still saying in earnest,
I must collect my pension before it
begins to rain.

Mango Tree

Conrad!
Conrad!
What you doing up there in
Mr Samuel's mango tree?
Who tell you to start picking de man'
'Julie' mangoes!
Garçon,
you should be on de wooden bus,
going to school,
not in de man' mango tree.

Get down from there boy,
before you fall,
it's only a young ting.
Conrad,
you listening to me,
you mashing up de mango tree,
you breaking it neck.
Get down boy!
So many mangoes mama buy for you
in de kitchen,
a large plastic bowl full of mango 'longs',
yet you still thiefing de man'
'Julie' mangoes.

Look Samuel coming, oui,
his face about to crack
like thunder.

Conrad!
Conrad!
You bring shame and disgrace on me.
After de man buy you an expensive bike
from America,
with all de latest gadgets,
and this is how you repay him.

Get down from that mango tree before
I break this broomstick on you.

MARTHA KAPOS

The Night Kitchen

Outside extinct stars hang
like scrunched-up letters thrown
around the floor. The earth is poised
on a hook above the sink.
An enormous sponge sits planetary and alone
in its enamel dish. So if I notice

a cracked glass face-down needs chucking out,
the draining-board is chipped by something
dropped last year, the forks all look
faintly yellow between their prongs —
why do my arms wrapped in mist in the Fairy Liquid
feel the long warm pull of the tide?

Why is it suddenly all
a darkness of islands in oceans, the inconstant soap
a slab of light slipping between my fingers
like a moon? And if the folded
dishcloth rises to a pinnacle of hope
against an embroidery of midnight-blue,

and if the bubbles coming on and going out
range themselves in a white ring big
as the Crab Nebula, and if I'm floating
inches above the ground, the pocket in my apron
growing into a pouch so large that it could hold
Medusa's head, J-cloths flapping

from my heels like the wings of Mercury,
and through the hazy half-dark I begin to see
a constellation in a drift of dust,
puddles on the floor big enough to hold the Milky Way —
will you keep the earth's poles

together between your firm hands, administer
the law of gravity, and hold onto all
the rattling atoms of the world?

Finding My Bearings

Such intricate
navigational equipment.
A search of the black sky

for the Pole Star. Soundings
to establish a safe depth.
Sailing in the dark up

the empty estuary, shining hotel
corridors with static
electricity in each doorknob.

Never go down teeteetum teeteetum
if you don't go down with me.
Why are the little roads

to your secret address so faint?
The *A to Z* of your smile without
getting lost. Its turnings and

mysterious co-ordinates.
Let's look it up
in the index under S:

Something Circus
Something Crescent
Something Close

JUDITH KAZANTZIS

Sunshine

A speed boat, a wake
like a silver-fish.

A wind like crowsfeet
treading the cloudback.

The pointed husks empty
of fronds and slowly waiting to fall off,

and sun, mad as the hatter,
eyes glinting through the blind slats

wherever my restless head twists
on the very pink pillow-slip,

that old sun gets to me.
I wrote 'she was so sweet'

while waiting — but in what
airport, what marina gifte shoppe —

for the word. That silver fish
slipped across the ocean like my kitchen floor —

I must sell up; so the word came.
O kitchen floor!

Very high up I lurched across someone else's
speedboat slewing across someone else's ocean

leaving that wake of a dolphin
of the kitchen. 'She was so sweet',

I wrote it like a mad palm-tree,
I shed, I fall off

and yes, you were, you flew to me
(I grow another, I fall off).

The Woods Of Balacet In The Pyrenees

for Alison Fell

We went into the woods of Balacet,
you and I,
picking flowers and the young limbs of trees,
green-leaved as giddy Eden
but we were frightened by an old man
who came for us with bolts,
rearing his iron tors
across the ungainly moorlands of the sky.

We crouched under the chestnuts and the beeches.
An owl sat on a post,
swivelling her stout neck, twirling
her feathers lacy with the calligraphics
of an ancient material.

We couldn't understand what she meant.
Whether the old man was really
green Pan,
playing the organ bass stops by mistake
and for a change…

But the more he roared at us STOP
in his guttural father's voice,
blue-black and travelling nearer
through the air, swollen with hunger
for the chestnuts, the ash-trees and the beeches,
the more you and I ran.

And so we left the woods of Balacet,
you and I,
and we lost the woods to the old man.

After A Life Time Together, Will Norma Ever Leave John?

The last of England. I wonder where it went.
Into the long grass beyond the cricket green.
A suit of armour sulking in a tent.

Flag and fox and stag and rose's scent,
us Norma people asking where we've been.
The last of England. I wonder where it went.

Thousands of us without an obvious bent,
us Norma people suddenly unseen,
A suit of armour sulking in a tent.

Years ago, you shyly said it meant
teatime, and vespers, and spinsters in between.
The last of England. I wonder where it went.

What luck it is to have no temperament,
A tear, no more, down history's latrine.
A suit of armour sulking in a tent,

still waiting to be told it's heaven sent
— us Norma people, that's rather not our scene.
The last of England. I wonder where it went.
A suit of armour sulking in a tent.

DAN KENNEDY

Theme Pub

Ceud mile failte
Welcome to the theme pub
Stations of the cross
I am Seamus Station
I'm the boss
Come on in
Tourist or refugee
Hear the Blarney
And the goosesteps
In synchronicity
Fancy a Joyce Walk
Or a talk on O'Casey
By the Abbey
Where we spat in his well
A very popular sight
In our virtual hell

I invented a culture
Drank it dry
Dug up the dead
Drained the maggots from their head
Dressed 'em up in ringlets
And called it dancin'
Historical traditional hysterical
I'm buildin' a hotel on the Hill of Tara
Landscape gardens artificial lakes
And I'm buyin' back the snakes
I'm cuttin' the drive
Through the ancient woods of the Celt
'Cause there's nothing like
Rippin' off yourself

Now I'm all speeded up
And the gravy train has run amok
And there is no level crossin'
And me head keeps turnin' and tossin'
In porter and fear
And I can't forget O'Casey
Sure there's no prostitutes here

Remember

Remember that morning in Camden
Love passion lust abandon
And the ash from the spliff
Fell on your breast
And I licked it clean
Soft touch on my chest
And we laughed ecstatically
Hands clenched to the stars
And the touch electrically
Sparks Venus and Mars
And you said the flat needed painting
And the coffee stained sheets needed fumigating

Remember?

The flat is now in red and green
The sheets are midnight blue and clean
And I'm no longer between
Day and night

But our love gave me a terrible fright

JOHN KERKHOVEN

Walk

Fingertips tingle with delicious cold.
Sun-diamonds twinkle on fresh snow.
Above the lake, solid with death-trap frost,
seagulls screech, Keee-ya! —
bright arrows crisscrossing blue.

Boots knerp-knerping spoors
across virgin white.
Dogs delighting jumping running —
sugar-snow mixes
with steam breath.

Steamed crowded café:
'Deux cafés, s'il vous plaît.'

Blossom

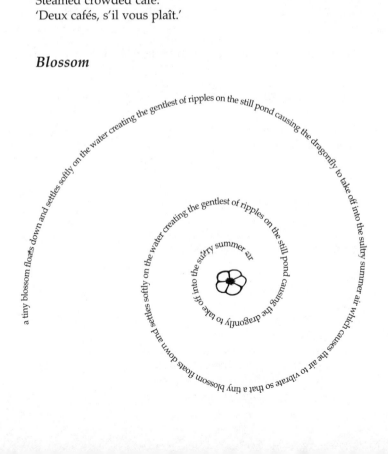

MIMI KHALVATI

Come Close

Think how beautiful we were to start with,
clear as glass. How impossible to part with,
stillness was a rope we tangled round
our mothers' hearts. In sleep we made no sound.

Come close the flower says and we come close,
close enough to lift, cup and smell the rose,
breathe in a perfume deep enough to find
language for it, and finding none, unwind

the rope back to a time before we knew
what we know now. When every word was true
and roses smelt divine. What went wrong?
Come closer still, close as the day is long.

Like a rose we slept in the morning sun.
Each vein a small blue river, each eyelash shone.

The Meanest Flower

I travel with aubretia, pansy, poppy,
seed anywhere and don't look back.
Let any wind sow me, any rough patch be
my home between the cracks.

Forget-me-not call me, if only, if only
memory grew in my tracks.
I blow at a window, away on a balcony,
straggle in moss round chimneystacks.

The child who stoops to examine me
— my stars, my spin of the zodiac —
will see, for every star in the galaxy,
there's one in the broken tarmac.

Give me a bombsite, wasteground, masonry,
fragment of history I'd otherwise lack.
Shallow my roots, sweet my taxonomy:
chickweed, speedwell, stonecrop, toadflax.

Don't Ask Me, Love, For That First Love
after Faiz Ahmed Faiz

Don't think I haven't changed. Who said
absence makes the heart grow fonder?
Though I watch the sunset redden
every day, days don't grow longer.

There are many kinds of silence,
none more radiant than the sun's.
Sun is silent in our presence,
unlike love, silent when it's gone.

I thought that every spring was you,
every blossom, every bud;
that summer had little to do
but follow, singing in my blood.

How wrong I was. What had summer
to do with sorrow in full spate?
Every rosebush, every flower
I passed, stood at a stranger's gate.

Weaving through our towns, centuries
of raw silk, brocade and velvet
have swilled the streets in blood. Bodies,
ripe with sores in lanes and markets,

are paying with their lives. But I
had little time for the world's wars,
love was war enough. In your sky,
your eyes, were all my falling stars.

Don't ask me, though I wish you would
and I know you won't, for more tears.
Why build a dam at *Sefid Rud*
if not to water land for years?

Though we'll never see the olives,
ricefields, shelter in an alcove
from the sun, in our time, our lives
have more to answer to than love.

ANGELA KIRBY

The New Painting

He calls it *Tulip* —
the paint splashes
across the thick paper,
drips and coagulates —
though the longer I look at it
the more it seems possible
that it is not a tulip
but a red moon
burning through white ice
or a warning light
or, more probably,
someone's bleeding heart
for last night it throbbed
in all my dreams
and today beats wildly
in a corner of the room.

The Sweet Scent of Hawthorn

You say the moon too is horned
but, as I see it from this angle, she is a raised eyebrow
and perhaps we have surprised her

for the cows too seem mildly astonished,
wide-eyed at our intricacies, chewing things over,
puzzled by such ineptitude.

They circle nearer, their broad flanks
hung with castanets of dung that click, click, click
to our quickening rhythm.

There is a lot of head-tossing and heavy breathing,
something sweet and foxy in the air,
our sweat brewing with the scent of hawthorn.

Making for the Lower Field

Hey oop! Hey oop!
We are making for the lower field,
the sun nothing more
than a gold rim round the distant elms.
Flicking at the paint,
I swing on the blue gate's hinge-end
as it whines open
and the shorthorns bucket through
in a reek of mud and hot shit,
oblivious to the future
which is staggering,
just so many holes in the head.

Hey oop! Hey oop!
I bang the pail, they come on by
amiably enough, these long-dead stirks
and heifers, over the plashed ground,
hips jaunty and gilded with pollen.
They swing pert heads
and roll their thick-lashed eyes,
still flirty under those veils
of may and elder — but look, now
they kick up their heels and rocket off,
high-tailing it into the sunset
while I limp on behind.

'There is strong evidence for the idea that memories are created afresh each time we experience them' (from a report on the application of Chaos Theory to human memory)

Night After Night

Grief? he said, turning away,
that's so pretentious...
but at nights, while he slept on
and it scoured into her skin
she found grief simple enough
and quite unaffected.

Death of the Ice Princess

Too late, they have come to visit her, to sort and tidy,
to parcel up her life, to brush and sweep away,

for this is where she died alone, under a shroud of dust.
It has taken over the house now, dulling the glass

and tortoiseshell, the photographs in silver frames,
the unopened letters that lie there in the hall,

muffling echoes, sealing up her books. Day after day,
lying there in bed, tracing patterns in the sad confetti,

shaking, shaking the mad kaleidoscope, she noted how
her skin dried, flaked, sloughed off, turned back to dust

as it filtered down the still air and then spun upwards
on a slant of light that pierced the tulip curtains

until at last she saw it grow bright as snow for one instant
when the sun caught it, sparkling in her hair

and on her lashes — *Ach, die Eisprinzessin* — and he called
to her, laughing, as he had called so long ago in St. Moritz,

when she came in from the night. Now, just before
the sudden darkness, as the motes burnt into her brain

and the iris of each eye, she saw him once again,
against that sky of comets, shooting stars and nebulae.

BERNARD KOPS

Isaac

Isaac came to a river.
It was so wide
he couldn't see the other side.

He didn't know where he was
or how he got there,

then he saw another boy
waving
swimming towards him.
He was beautiful.
What's your name the swimmer said
emerging...

I have no name he laughed.
Then we shall call you Isaac
the swimmer said.
It means laughter.

And so Isaac became Isaac.
What's this river called? Isaac asked.
This river is called life.
My name is Max the swimmer said.
Now we must get to the other side.
I can't swim I'm only just born, Isaac replied.

Jump on my back Max commanded.
I am your brother. I'll take you across.
And Max laughed and laughed
and Isaac laughed and laughed
and their laughter joined together
and echoed all across the water
as they made for the other shore.

Barbara

Nothing that was said
in that room you left behind
to commemorate your death
brought me to tears.

I had not known you long
but of course I felt your loss.
There was a certain beauty
and goodness about you,
an innocence. A timelessness.

No. Not even the tears
in all those congregated eyes
moved me to really
feel the loss.

It was a note to your daughter
from a school friend,
consoling her with straight
pure kindness.
Written so simply
with such stark beauty,
those now forgotten words struck me,
caused me to hurry away
into the swimming road outside.

Your Trousers

Your trousers are ready Erica said
I've taken them up an inch or so.
You've shrunk a little
But even so
Your head it seems continues to grow.
Are you listening my love? Did you ever?
Were you ever prepared for inclement weather?
Your trousers are ready Erica said.

So I took them off and got into bed.

LOTTE KRAMER

Exodus

For all mothers in anguish
Pushing out their babies
In a small basket

To let the river cradle them
And kind hands find
And nurture them

Providing safety
In a hostile world:
Our constant gratitude.

As in this last century
The crowded trains
Taking us away from home

Became our baby baskets
Rattling to foreign parts
Our exodus from death.

Library Men

Those library men
In deep conversation
With dailies and weeklies,
They sit there and gossip
To out-of-work shadows,
They chuckle, they grumble,
They brood in aloneness,
In tweeds and in denims
And a jury of books.

Ex-India, 1940's

Quite shabby-elegant, in khaki army
Cast-off clothes, still from his India years,
Retired now, he'd totter round the house
Inspecting black-out curtains for a pleat

Of light, or feeding, talking to the cats,
As lack of conversation made him odd.
Somewhere there had been a sharp intellect
Submitted though to discipline and drill.

He would, in winter, carry in one hand
A paraffin-stove from room to smallest room,
Sometimes as laughing stock for younger eyes.
Perhaps there was an ogre buried in his youth,

Fear of neglect or an outsider's stealth
And he would rave and shout for trivialities.
A hypochondriac, he cured himself
With Christian Science terminologies.

But when his wife lay prostrate on the floor
After a stroke, he closed the door —
He sat and prayed beside her day and night
And no one knew or came until too late.

PHILIPPA LAWRENCE

Windows Of The Soul

A couple of days before my mother's soul
left her body
the windows of it clouded over.
Her eyes stared from open lids
as through opaque glass:
marbles in the pallid face
breathing laboriously on the hospital pillow.

Were they really unseeing
or just unseen;
the blinds pulled down,
the resident peeking from behind?
Blank eyes no longer glaring
anger, distain, jealousy, threats —
snake with rabbit
instilling eternal apprehension
and low self esteem
which unintentionally bred
shame at my lineage,
being of her blood.

It was no comfort
to see the ogre brought low;
a powerless form
attached to morphine and catheter tubes;
warm hands limp,
unable to grasp or spank or shake me.
She lay vanquished, immobile
yet I could not rejoice,
felt no triumph —
her near lifelong chipping away
at my soul and confidence
ceasing only as death approached.

At last her torso rose up,
jerking briefly to a sitting position,
eyes staring blindly;
then she flopped back on the pillow,
harsh breathing stopped,
her soul flown to that place below
from the now harmless body,
her eyes still gazing
through milky glass, darkly.

I can feel no grief
except for what might have been
had she remained the kind companion and teacher
of my first four happy years
whose soft hazel eyes looked on me
with delight and loving pride.
I kissed the dead brow gently
as once she used to bid
her sleeping little girl
a final, lingering goodnight.

SARAH LAWSON

One Afternoon In Fuzhou

The street runs uphill toward a dusty sun
Still tropically hot in September.
Ahead of us a young man stops his bike to talk
To a seamstress in her sidewalk shop.
He is forgetting about his fish in the box
On the back of his bike.
His meal sees its chance and squirms over the side,
Then flopping sideways on the street
It makes a dash for it,
This plucky dying fish,
Hoping a river lies somewhere opposite.
We politely show the man his carp is about to be
A flatfish.   We are helpful and foolish
In equal measure, ridiculously
Apprehending an escaping fish
Now in the middle of a trafficked street
With its keeper in hot pursuit,
The seamstress watching, wondering (I wonder)
If she wants to marry a man
Who lets his fish get run over,
And the man obliged to chase his carp
Among the bikes and trucks
Under the eyes of his seamstress,
Who is never again going to look at him
Without a smile that will remind him of his blasted fish.

Leda

My wings are strong enough to break
A man's leg, you know. I could take
One good swipe with my splendid wing,
One strong stroke would be enough.
He'd be down before he knew a thing
After my solid swan-wing cuff.

A swaggering swan is a sight to see.
As he bragged to Leda about how he
Was so strong, he invaded her private space.
She avoided an attempted peck.
She gazed firmly into his face,
Reached out and wrung his neck.

Visit My Website

Visit my website, said the spider to the fly,
Let me see your sonsie interface
Among the growing cyberzoo
Here in deepest cyberspace
Where chips fall where they may, and thick,
And mice no longer squeak but click.

Don't, pray, be so outmoded
As to resist my charm.
Would I do you any harm?
Don't you want to be downloaded?

MARGARET LEFF

Jack in a Box

1.
Jack
Doesn't want
To be in the box.

A moment of glory
A leap into space:

Then shoved down
And the lid shut tight.

2.
His hat was squashed
In the hot stuffy box.

He pushed and shoved
With all his might.

Nil desperandum
He cried...

When a chubby finger
Released him

Allowing his great
Leap into light.

EDDIE S. LINDEN

The Miner

for my Father

Your face has never
moved, it still contains
the marks of toil, deep in
blue. These slag heaps
now in green have
flowers instead of dust
and many men are buried here
whose shadows linger on.

For a Dublin Artist

for John Behan

He works in bronze creating matter
in steel
Not like those who sit in judgement with jars
of Guinness.
I have seen them on high stools passing out
unpublished work
While someone labours into the night amid the lightning flash
of a welder's rod.

His is not just of brain as of brawn.
Nor do you find a man in idle talk with fools
in intellectual bars
Only in the gallery will you find the finished piece
and find the man.

The Man in the Black Suit

He didn't want me to ask too many questions
The coffee warmed his cold body
His Glasgow accent was clear
The black suit gave away the secret
of what he had done in the past.
The drink had reduced his spirit for life
It was all in the face
The shoes years old
A torn prayerbook in his pocket.

The Concert

for Lloyd Orchard

Music is what he lives by
He directs his pen and we wait for the finished piece
The subject he has thought long
His time is limited
Do not distract him until he calls back.
From outside his room comes the sound of music,
You know he's getting there, he will call a taxi
And deliver the end product.

The vodka bottle is back on the table and the concert goes on.

DINAH LIVINGSTONE

Ygdrasil

Ygdrasil in Camden Town,
uptwisting trunk great sycamore,
from my terrace I greet you early,
your crown curves so generously
against the new day's sky.
The rising sun lights your big body
and strikes the spiral iron fire escape
on the brick flats to your left,
so that its shadow shapes a double helix,
solid and ephemeral, as London wakes.
I look out over sheds, which gardeners
are about to visit to get their tools,
to where you stand in the park.
Soon a few old drunks will come
to sit on the tombstone at your foot,
argue politics with alcoholic logic,
scuffling from time to time.
Meanwhile, from the main road,
the muffled rush-hour roar picks up —
wildlife active to survive —
as, some still half asleep,
they thrust their way to work.

Ygdrasil, late afternoon
the sun comes round behind you
so that your leaves are now translucent.
I gaze from my terrace wrought-iron chair
surrounded by reddening autumn vines —
so many and such sweet grapes this year;
for me, much stress, frustration
but I've done some difficult work
I'm glad about. A resting body now
I nod to the delicate little cyclamen
in their big pots of plain earthenware
and sip pale yellow wine.
I look up. Ygdrasil,
I see your glory in the golden light.
You have clothed the sun in living green.

Breaking through it dazzles me.
I am in the heart of London and remember
Blake saw an angel
in a tree at Peckham Rye.

At 3 am I wake in darkness
troubled by slithering anxieties
shifting between global and domestic,
confusing images, noises of war.
I go out on the terrace and I see
stars muted by the crowding city
yet still their heavenly multitude.
Most of the houses round me are asleep.
Perhaps tonight in one of those dark rooms
a new life will be conceived.
Just the occasional lit window.
Maybe someone battling on with work
or woken too like me.
Over Ygdrasil,
complete with mountains visible,
the full moon beams down
silvering your black profile,
your strong presence like a ghost,
overflowing me with stillness and the sense
of Earth as a body needing peace,
herself a modest sphere in space
turning towards new day.

ALEXIS LYKIARD

White Thoughts

Procrastination is the thief of time — Edward Young (*Night Thoughts*, 1744)

Ejaculation is the thief of time,
a plentiful and urgent sneeze of loins,
blindingly pleasurable though petty spasm.

You make it new through unrelenting thrust,
and next will come relief, the end of lust.
For dawdlers with finality, addictive slime

sticks all together, flaws and follies, joins
fantasy, *amour fou* and loneliness.
Welcome appearance as bright trick or truth,

mindless it spurns the ache of age and youth:
instinctive creatures may thereby express
a quite consuming joy and dreadfulness.

So we repeat each fleeting little death,
forestall with seemingly triumphal breath
that last gasp of a brief life's phantasm!

Tag from Terence

humani nihil a me alienum puto

Go up the garden path,
gravely over gravel,
to note what this day brings.
Riches indeed: a trio
of fat slugs. All crawl
avid across a pile
of very recent cat-sick…

While binning the whole
scooped old olio,
one's moved to recall
the role of literary critic
and vile tide of quasi-solid
sludge these slimy things
are given to feed on.

THOMAS McCOLL

Muslim Girl At The Bus Stop

Muslim girl at the bus stop
wearing hejab and headphones,

full length skirt and colourful top,
respecting Allah and listening to hip-hop,

the fingers of her left hand
click to the beat of the tune,

the fingers of her right hand
 adjust the veil, keep it in place,

covering her hair
and perfectly framing her beautiful face.

SUE MACINTYRE

Walking With Him

Richard's photographs

The Eiffel Tower in a bird's nest,
underwater autumn leaves wrapped in cellophane.
You're teasing us.

The gardener's become a ghost;
gravestones with lichen blots
are somehow faceless rabbits and bears;
an ancient chestnut trunk's
a puckered, sagging, warty face.

Maine rocks can soften into flesh —
creases, pleats, sunlit folds.
Here's abandoned ship's tackle
like tumbled vertebrae in mist:
your teasing eye.

And beyond teasing —
your voice changes gear to an insistent whisper —
look in, look in —
there's a pun here, an eye pun —
for this instant it's rock and flesh.

Or you're showing us moments of crossover —
cross-dressing of one element with another:
dry/wet, wet/dry,
as if the glittering rock face
in an old slate mine is trying to
stream down in a waterfall,
or leaves reflected in blue water
want to freeze into
the lid of an enamelled box,
or the panels of polished steel
on a New York building become
a watery sheet with wild distortions —
traffic floating in the sky,
smudges of elongated neon signs.

A birch tree in winter flowers
in a haze of minuscule water drops,
hinting it's spring — like the flicker
of a distant relative caught on a child's face.

Or you give us a magic peepshow
through a crevice in a roughened marble wall.
You say bend down, slow down, look
through the tiny triangle.
There's a miniature temple in the space,
a treasure, disguised at first, hard to find.
You've found it.

And you show us something moving across something still
like cloud shadows over a landscape —
the living passing like clouds over the dead,
the dead passing like clouds over the living.

Paper Thin

for my mother

The car's waiting.
We are the other side of the big unchanging space
of pale gravel chips.
We call out to you — are you all right?

Your face is intent on where you're going,
its folds strong like crumpled white paper.
You hold your handbag and walk forward tenaciously
but seem to be moving backwards
into the dark pines.

RICHARD McKANE

'A headache developing'

A headache developing.
This morning I saw a fluid
jagged line in the air.

Nazim Hikmet is not all enveloping.
There's space left for the Celtic Druid,
Judaeo-Christianity and Islam's flare.

War in Israel and Palestine,
Afghanistan, soon perhaps Iraq.
It screws up the intestines
and makes your lower back ache.

From blows to the head it gives you epilepsy
and feeds you Western lines of coke and ecstasy
till you are oh so hyper-hyper,
like the flitting tongue of a viper.

In Memory Of Tom Landau

Now I no longer need to be your interpreter
for I think you understand all rather than nothing:

those snatches of conversation in many languages
of the throng on the black tarmac under the black sky
that threatened downpour. Grief and pain you understood
intuitively and treated. Now you understood the bearded Kurd
when he agreed with me in Turkish: 'He is a very happy man'
'Chok nesheli bir adam': to keep it in the present made perfect
grammatical sense. But in English I kept slipping you into the past tense.
Wrong really, for you were very present that day, and are with me today,
three dimensional, in this time even too, in this England,
in that passage in Eliot's *Little Gidding 5*
that Elizabeth combed out in grief like a daughter
in laughter and grief might comb your strong white hair.

We could have read that timeless poem of time
and strive to believe that 'All manner of things will be well',
but I felt a caution as you worked the crowd at your formal farewell:
a little spirit here, a little spirit there,
as though your work was far from completed.
No, you were not putting in extra hours at the Medical Foundation,
you were not on holiday in Simi,
or entertaining friends in your spacious home,
but you are somewhere: I know that since you are not here.
I don't know why I felt you in my
mind's eye floating in the sky
looking huge and looking down on us,
for you seemed to be already filling within us the vacuum of your loss.
And now I realise again how much
time, space and memory the special dead occupy:
how many of that crowd is solemnly bound in your death
to treat the torture which it is widely believed ends with death.

But I see you with your stethoscope and little reflex stick
in a small room filled, alas, with our stereophonic pipe smoke,
working at the end of a long session the individual in our intimate
triangle into health with the interpreted verbal pinprick of:
'Now for English *falaka*' and you tap the *falaka'd* feet
under calves that have suffered the tight rings of 'English sock torture'.
I see you feeling with that peculiar blend of amusement out loud
and silent sympathy through the hirsute forest
of a Kurdish chest for hairline scars,
and recording the notes in silent hand that you alone could read.
Since you so valued silence, and a look that penetrated without
disturbing the soul, it is easier for me to take your silence.
I see you now, and almost hear in the new way now I will have to hear
your Blues Guitar, gravelling out your 'Discrepancy Blues'.
Oktay Rifat in his elegy and lament to Orhan Veli
said 'Come, come my brother Orhan, take my hands, use my eyes':
but you gave words to translate, and enrolled me as
'more than an interpreter'; so as a good interpreter remembers
a long speech, I retain your words to pass on,
your body language, your intention and fortitude,
your anger against injustice.
Once it was word for word,

but now I carry over on the memory of you,
I guess I am still your interpreter.

But I started to write this poem, Tom,
after it woke me at dawn, to tell you,
not only of death — you know that secret now — but love,
of family loving at the sharp edge of human love,
of friends, of comrades, of the people you treated so well.
There were so many people there, Tom,
that Elizabeth and I had to stand at the back.
The Turkish artist's baby was not the only one who cried,
'You're tearing too' an interpreter said graphically.
But though torn with English tears
Elizabeth and I hugged for us as well as you.
It was all you, it is all you:
we'll fight suffering and death with memories and love.

KATHLEEN McPHILEMY

Umbilical

At two o'clock in the morning
the phone rang again;
the voice was drunk or distraught.

Yes, I told him, we know;
yes, we've already heard
and the voice went away.

He must have been on a mobile
he didn't know how to use:
he stopped, but the line stayed open.

Over or under the sea
across the billowing darkness
sounds of grief in a kitchen:

the clatter of cups of tea
a door that opened and closed
breathless sentences, half-spoken.

I tried to shout down the phone,
I tried to break the connection;
I tried, but the line stayed open.

Losing The Plot

When I visit the allotment now
I no longer see work in progress
I see it as work abandoned.

Fragments — a strawberry paragraph
indecipherable, faded to brown;
leafless lines of raspberries
sprawling, unpruned, dead wood.

Halfway up the page
is a rhyming couplet of leeks,
still neat, but etiolated
enough for a pauper's soup.

The door of the shed's fallen off;
it gapes like an open mind,
cluttered with broken tools
and empty compost sacks —

things that might one day be useful
and a wheelbarrow to take them away in.

Failure Of Imagination

Another hour ticked through; the boiler flares,
pipes expand and the house creaks towards morning.
As daylight builds behind the curtain,
the first bird, hesitant, spills into song.
Though I know he's too old to keep tabs on,
I listen all night for the key in the door.
My fears are unspecific, like the wailing siren,
ambulance or police, that screams past the end of the street.

By day, I feel a spurious security:
the postman with his red bike doesn't alarm me,
I hardly hear the planes that pass overhead;
the air smells fresh, the newsprint is dry and clean
as I read with angry pity of all those other
children scrabbling in the dust of their bombed-out lives.

Talking Politics

I sat at the table between them
as day receded from the garden
at the hour of early dusk.

I was silent; they were speaking:
there was only one story that night
and the way they told it was different.

They were men with powerful faces,
lines reinforced on their cheeks
by thirty years of unchanged opinions.

The room was full of obscurities
but light and dark waxed eloquent
on the strength of their polished convictions.

E. A. MARKHAM

from *Epic*

Ceremony at Maracuene, Mozambique

The Animal Pound and flower bed
back home
were round. The bronzed cistern

breeding froglife
at the back of the house
seemed the right shape.

From boxing ring and track
to the call it Stadium
we all worship in the round.

And what new marvel
(Mr. Marco Polo & Columbus)
you bringing back now

from your travels?—
for already it have calabash and Zulu-
hut safe in the museum.

Nothing, man, nothing
but a chance meeting under a tree
in a place I can't remember.

No jump-up and foolishness;
all low-key and calm
man, woman dress-up for they thing.

'Nuf to say it shape like
something ancient. Quiet quiet.
No applause. Sky-henge. Magic.

from *Epic*

She would, wouldn't she, call your bluff,
great scourge of a grandmother
too many years gone to confront
except in jest. (Yes, you'll remember
to ring the Mother and help
nieces with their homework; all that.)
But no, her beady eye that
never needed glasses dims now
like yours to let you wriggle out of
hearing a question old as the gospels:
are you, boy, still stupid or crazy?
Lack of answer hints of end to
this game of talking to the dead.

Is there someone, still, to convince
you might be on the right side
of a cause? Just last night, with friends
you condemned this man in the news
his strange use of words, like honour
and friendship turning one of you
into a foreign speaker. But
he's far away from knowing that
he spoilt your dinner-party. So,
who will force apology for this
use of language we can't live by?
That man, neither stupid nor crazy,
good at what he does, outwits you daily.

Reunion

We don't trust them; they indite us.
Brother Eugene doesn't attend

for whatever reason. Others less
house-weary have died since last time.

And yet to see this event the Lourdes &
Compostella of the clan

reduced to three stragglers
whose names we can't pronounce

is a slap in the face for
Ancestors who planned dynasty.

Though Lindsay is family still,
divorced or not, bringing back a whiff

of America to grace our house.
But these new refugees from London

don't look or sound like us: a joke
against pioneers stranded there

since the unforgiving last
century. At least the good doctor

serving the drinks, son of a long-
time retainer pulls rank enough

to spare family blushes.
So, what now? As they move on from

verandah to dining-room
they tell the stories you might expect:

triumph over adversity.
Family trees that grow in rough

climate. Raised glasses. Absent friends.
And where are you now, my brother?

JEHANE MARKHAM

The Blue Apron

A strange, rare thing hung in a glass case,
Like an open wing
It was a shroud,
Mended *ad infinitum*
The distilled rising of a cloud,
Butterflies bearing up the dead.
How did this map of tenderness survive?
A patchwork apron strung out between pins
Hewn with a needle and thread.
An old Gestapo *Kino* plays films about Terezin.
For what I did not know, I cannot mourn
Yet unformed words are beginning to form...
It was as pale as dried cornflowers,
Bleached to a gossamer sail in places,
The stitches like train tracks over blue fields.

Valentine

Knowing love as I really think I really
Do, I sometimes laugh like a baby seeing
Faces turn to and turning home to faces
    Lovely and yearning.

Love is always returning home to its
Sources, finding pathways and backward winding
Seams of water, divining rods and streams
    Uprising purely.

Turn me to you, then, surely, without loss of
Face, for heaven is only what we long for
Accidentally, face to face, childlike sometimes
    True as a swan-song.

The Tenant

Without his mother's voice to chide,
This man has gone beyond his past,
The crystal waves, oncoming tide.

One cup alone by teapot's side,
Tea towels strung along the mast,
Without his mother's voice to chide,

He mopes for something lost, denied.
Meals on wheels arrive at last,
The crystal waves, oncoming tide.

It was a Saturday she died,
Always the tears fall thick and fast,
Without his mother's voice to chide.

The books he keeps as friends, beside,
Are Dickens, Tennyson and Proust.
The crystal waves, oncoming tide.

A man's history lives inside,
But death will come too slow, too fast,
Without his mother's voice to chide,
The crystal waves, oncoming tide.

NANCY MATTSON

Ceremony Of Eels

A winter break, a week without
the shallownine to dryfives for me;
all my friend from Lapland wants
is anything but snow, dark, trees.

We walk slow and local, inhale
the barny smells of cheeses,
gaze at pig snouts and tails
dried scarlet at the market, flinch

at eels writhing in the eel pie
and mash shop window, each
constricted by a pale white hairy
hand, the body twitches

while a set of pale white hairy
fingers grips the knife, aims
quick at the point where bare
neck would be if bulbous head

were any part of eelness.
It is not. The eel is shorter
dead, but still a long thing,
now sliced along a thin line

from blooded top to tapered tail
by windowed hands abstracted
from the eelmonger, torso
disembodied by his task, matter, fact.

Walking The Line

What I miss is gravel
crunching under foot or wheel,
wide sky above
the road straight into horizon.

I want to walk the crease
of a prairie book, lines of wheat
as even type, all one size
the word gold over and over.

London's a fused maze
of alphabets: wherever you walk,
each road, wherever it turns,
is utterly paved or cobbled crookedly.

A crazed typesetter has been at work
every night for centuries, his head
swirling with shadows thrown
on crumbling walls by candle-flame.

He has set every line diabolical
in a different font and size,
hot lead in higgledy-piggledy frames
and gutters overflowing with errata.

Waltz Of The Wyverns

Slyly they murmur   mild-eyed maidens
whisper to the walls   their heartlocked wishes
deep in the City's   dungeons of drudgery
neatthroated nightingales   number their days

Under the eaves   the elders of earnestness
toilmakers endless   with tedious tautology
milksoppy limp-leggèd   memomakers sitabout
dictating pages   and pages of pettypap

Ho! for the flowcharts   fatuous flapdoodle
bureaucrats' bumfodder   piled up in boxes
bossdriven bosses   blind to their servitude
palefaced   pencilpushers
browknitted   branchheads
upwardly mobile   minions and mendicants
whine in one voice   *In Valium veritas*

Perching above   pillars and porticoes
wonderful wyverns   weavers of song
and glorious griffins   guardians of joy
so lithe in their lays   so lissom their limbs
rise to the stirrings of   sweetthroated maidens
and waltz them away   on spelldriven wings

GERDA MAYER

Beowulf — A Riposte

My name is Mrs Grendel,
There is a pub next door
Whose racket is a scandal;
My son gave them 'what for'.

Their closing time was Never.
We told them to shut up:
They thought it mighty clever
When I was quite cut up.

They said we lived in squalor,
They said we were the pits:
They gave us plenty dolour
Those empty-headed Gits!

We moved into the cellar
And still could hear their din.
There was that foreign feller
Who did my poor boy in.

They claimed, in mitigation,
That it was self-defence;
And great was their elation,
When pardoned the offence.

In *Beowulf*, the story,
The pub was called *The Hart*,
It does not tell how, truly,
They tore us quite apart.

They called us whingers, ogres
And wrote it down as said:
Their story is quite bogus
Although it's been much read.

*In the Anglo-Saxon poem, Beowulf the Geat vanquishes the monsters Grendel
and Grendel's mother who harried the thanes in the mead hall Heorot (The Hart)
and lived at the bottom of a lake.*

Snapshots

My poems are snapshots.
They catch
the moment's truth only.
Tomorrow my mood
will blow from a different quarter,
bend the facts
another way.

A Young Man Leaning Against A Tree Among Roses

Nicholas Hilliard's Miniature in the Victoria and Albert Museum

He leans against a tree, his head
Served on a platter of white lace;
A man for Charis — locks surround his face*.

His pensive air among the leaves evokes
The age of poesy in this little oval;
The stance a courtier's: setting pastoral.

Roses like sonnets grow across his cloak.
Unforced, yet trim, with such spontaneous art —
And so stands he — his hand upon his heart.

Ben Jonson's 'To Charis/Her Answer'

Don't Give A Fairy The Cold Shoulder

for children

Don't give a fairy the cold shoulder.
Be respectful to the spook upon the stairs.
If you hob-nob with Hobgoblin,
Be careful not to snub him,
For hobgoblins tend to take you unawares.

Don't give a fairy the cold shoulder.
Be indulgent to a poltergeist and seek
Not to make a face too sour
When he thumps upon the hour,
For a pixy can be tricksy though antique.

Don't give a fairy the cold shoulder.
Pay the magician with applause.
For a wizard has a wand
Which will waft you to Beyond,
Where you'll be a gnome for Santa Claus.

MARY MICHAELS

Shift

Between land and sea
there are gabion defences
wire netting cages
packed tight with stones

but the beach is still
eroding underneath them
like a tooth being worn away
around a filling

Two rows of children
stand in front of glass cubes
watching shelves of two-pence pieces
being shunted under spotlights

in the gleam
their faces are illuminated

the game is
waiting for some pence to slip
for the cliff to crumble

A boy begging comes along the bus
he's about nine, round faced
in a thick jumper
with rough hair, grimy

I'm not going to give

but his face mimes
such an expression of desperate need
that I dig into my purse
and pull out a pound
for his polystyrene cup

the coin is the same dull gold
as the boy.

Fugue

Nothing can be heard but the water's rush
pushing of waves over waves over stones

the sea, all in movement, looks as fixed
as the churned-up earth of a rain-wet plain
unclaimed, unfenced

There is a way to be made across
to the far edge of all that space

A straight road
it seems to be saying

a day's walking
even half a day

Tall clouds, gunmetal grey
are growing out of that wide horizon
playing at mushrooms, forests, mountains

and I am ready to walk the sea.

Indistinct

Eight in the morning
strong wind
        bright sun

only one or two people
            along the beach

Where sky and milk blue sea line meet

a shape
        not Island
        not car ferry

big for that distance
and as dark as it was white

Something not right about this thing
moving leftwards
in eye-blinks
            slowly

outline that couldn't be identified
and looked as if it might
            turn the whole sea up

raise it vertical

Only an act of will from me
could keep that water a horizontal sea
with waves harmlessly running in.

JOAN MICHELSON

Harvest

Hour after hour, I wake to moon
sharpening shadows in my cabin window.
You too recall the harvest scythes
and the summer of our wandering.

We slept all together in the barn
working towards our passage home
not wanting, not ever, the season's end.
I keep dreaming of that ending and wake

to moon pouring through my cabin window.
It's the end of summer. I hear the fiddle
in the birch trees bent by wind scraping
branches against branches for the dance.

I hear the harvest singing and see myself
with blade beheading pale dry stalks
as if they're creatures and we're one with them.
I'm still cutting when the trees are flaming.

Flying

I keep seeing you off

— half asleep in Costa Coffee
checked in for Moscow,

in high sun on Egged
out of Tel Aviv,

now in Florence, Prague.

This time it's nearly spring.
Again you're headed east.

Should I keep flying out and in
like this? Stork or wild turkey?

No. More unwieldy.
A creature without wings.

In a picture, recent,
I caught you seated

underneath a shelf.
You eyes were closed.

A mother wonders
what a daughter feels.

Just a bit choppy I hear
until we get our altitude.

DAVID MILLER

Poem

for Faith

Augustine in despair
beholds his own face
(his life); a child cries,
Take up and read. He reads;
he changes. I too turn
right round. Your face
before me rewrites my sight.

Spiritual Letters

(Series 3, #2)

Sitting at a small table on the balcony, drinking wine and
writing draft after draft by lamplight. More and more inca-
pacitated, his head snapping backwards in spite of himself, the
boy was stranded in the waiting room. Having dropped the
heap of leaves, the little girl beseeched her sister and parents
to help her pick them up again. — You should try writing a
novel, he told me. *Dear is the honie that is lickt out of thornes.*
Desire's thrown into confusion; overwhelmed. Full moon
above trees in the long window. Stepping down — plunging
into water. The stranger he'd been gazing at earlier suddenly
came over to speak to him and fetched a nurse, insisting he
should be looked after immediately; her compassion caught
him, so unexpected.

Spiritual Letters

(Series 3, #3)

To be sung: ...*that the lost might life inherit*... A sheet draped over the chair. We sat at a table between two banana plants, a pool of water gathering underneath. A banner of flame in the night sky, above the treetops and streetlights. In a shop on the way to her home, she chose a circular mirror for me to purchase; in another shop, fuchsias for herself. I dreamt that the artist — most famously narcissistic of her generation — had died; yet later in the dream I encountered her at a private view. The old woman turns a radio on at the back of the lecture hall, loud static interrupting the discussion. He arrived at my door, his suitcase full of fish bones. On the far wall of the living room, a sheet was draped around the mirror. Between the twin rocks, a reddish light — as if scumbled over the pond's surface. — *A good amulet,* he said, invoking, gathering protection. The small silver hand was engraved with letters, signs. — The motherfuckers won't let me sing, the woman said at her friend's funeral. Around the frame, a pattern of stars, or the names of angels.

C. D. MORGAN

Dark Matter

Came across the Afrikaans
    verligte again the other day.
Politically passé now maybe,
    but then meaning what?

In the chiaroscuro of the politics
    of Africa and the Enlightenment,
What did they have to say
    of the slavery of memory, person or tradition?

What do they have to say now
    when everyone twists
To take advantage of the emotional import
    of each unillumined concept?

As words fly quicker than the grounded planes,
Emptier than business class of any reason,
Is this the time of incandescent feeling?

Can the dark soul be illumined,
Or are we for ever to be made of the dark matter
Only newly theorised?

Love Superannuated

Next Spring

> Flowers in the garden,
> Silhouette on the park bench,
> Reminder of love.

Winter Before

> Convoluted tree.
> We used to sit under it.
> Chopped down now. Empty.

Autumn Before Last Spring

> Leaves swirled in the gale.
> Dazzled by the rising sun,
> Said 'Hello,' and ran.

Last Spring

> Saw her through the trees,
> Smile on unknown face approached.
> Argument connects.

SHARON MORRIS

Sitting On The Fence

A cow looks at the world over a fence.

The camera sees differently.

If I shut my eyes the world stays there.

When you saw the round owl
    looking at you — where was I?

A goldcrest, round like a ping-pong ball,
    beak stuck on impromptu, sings on top
then under a twig, decking its flame head.

The way you told me, how you felt the rock
    pools breathing, stays with me — more persistent
than my own perceptions.

    Red flowers, red berries, fire-weed, I know
now, mark the infinite field of green—
    infinite degrees of yes and no.

Categorical Heart

Perhaps the universe splits at each event.
Either you're here with me, or

you're not, isn't then so simple.
And the difference between forgiveness and forgetting?

It has its logic, the heart, four cavities
the exchange of blood and oxygen.

I look at the sway of poplar trees,
listen to the wood pigeon — an oboe.

As one thing leads to another
the taste of tamarisk comes, heedless, and I think.

Memory is a phenomenon of the present
and not the past.

There's the old man walking his dog again.
He stops, attaches the lead, and picks him up.

Sometimes a fight for life lasts only moments:
not the man you saw in Victoria Park, ablaze.

It's like that, listening to the heart.

ROSEMARY NORMAN

Down's Child

He bears her like a trophy,
riding his shoulders
above the nodding crowd
whose daughters ask
for no more than the moon.

But he is offering to her
the gaudy sun, forever,
and three guitars
that jangle old songs
now, in the town square.

She takes the beams, full
on her winged eyelids,
and in some raucous tale
of separated hearts,
can listen to perfection.

Writing Behaviour*

I slept well in the hospital
and dressed and ate
cleanly at the proper time.

My replies were apposite
civil and even. Yet
there was the matter of the notes.

I see myself under the window
(my chair is of tube steel)
and discolouring plastic)
and I am aware of the light
into which I lean back
and the ends of my hair
stand up in millions of tiny
separate glows, and the brightness
travels along my writing arm and down
the one leg that is crossed over
the other (the knee, the notebook)

and I am making notes
which may be no more than my name
written till I perfect it, written
over itself and over the notebook's
edges and over my shirt and trousers
and over my face and the fronts
and backs of my hands
till the whole of me is written
over myself, and I
can slip out of it and they think
they still have me, but I
am leaving, leave it behind me
in the shape of me, and I go.

* *...as part of an experiment, some American researchers had themselves
confined in an asylum masquerading as schizophrenics. In hospital, those
pseudo-patients behaved normally, on occasion taking written notes of what they
observed. The action was noted in their case histories as symptomatic of their
schizophrenia: it was called 'engaging in writing behaviour'.* — *Roy Porter,
A Social History of Madness.*

Duet

As their fingers thicken on zips
and hooks, the notes unpattern.

Drop by drop there was rain, now
it sheets the window. The violin

lifting its slim neck, the piano
testing its sturdy heart, they move

together through fine modulations
of touch, deep into dissolution.

....

After sleep, they stroke the darker
passages from one another's ears.

All day, in the white hiss of rain
they go under cover of music.

NICK ORENGO

Shall The Dead Speak

And shall the dead dream of heaven as the winds dream their colours
Careless as stars unadored on their high altars burning;
And shall they speak as men anywhere on the prosceniums of streetcorners,
Sharp and bright as a toyshop of light and its jackinabox midsummer grief;
I say they will turn like electrons on the singing coin, and wit
Angled strange as moonlight; on acts of love committed thoughtlessly
As crimes in foreign lands; the troubled prayer-dark sleep at dawn that is
the temptation
Of angels, and an idiot laughing at the lightning of God's smile
within the storm.
Shall the dead rise like poppies from green damned regions,
Or as celandines upon the grasses of the nowhere of paradise;
I say they shall speak like wicked soapbox orators blessed
With the clear, stinging, never-fallen rain of grace, from gutters, steeples
And urinals, somewhere between lost continents of memory and air
That all who suffer sins gladly and with patience
May bear their burdens lightly as leaves bled in murderous Autumn.

WILLIAM OXLEY

So You Write Poetry?

'So you write poetry?'
he made it sound like something
the police could get you for.
'Well, what's the use of that?
Let me tell you something —
most people can do it
and rhyme it as well,
which you don't seem able to do.

'But back to my question:
what's the use of it?
Can it win wars?
More likely lose them!
Of course, you'll say it's about love?
Well, I expect women like it.
But where's the money in it?'
There isn't any, I can tell you!
And where's the fame?
None — unless you're dead
and what use is that?
Better be a footballer or politician
or a really criminal criminal,
if it's fame you want.

'No, let's face it, poetry won't
unstop a blocked drain,
start a broken-down car,
fix a bust washing machine,
cook a decent meal,
cure any sort of illness,
win you a bet on a horse,
keep you out of trouble
(though it might get you into it!).
It's just a hobby and
a funny one at that, I'd say.

'In fact, it's a waste of time
and that's harmful

for time's money and time's life
and neither should be wasted,' he concluded
turning on the television.

The Ward

On every side the sound of suffering
(beyond the blinds another wind)
surrounded, as I say, by human wrecks
with fear on fear in every mind.

In life, in death we're patients all
in health and sickness just the same
yet still the mystery none can crack
what really is the meaning of the game?

They come in here the wasted men
like gone-off fish with awful coughs;
yet most are soon about again,
fears hidden under bantering laughs.

The doctors do it, of course, we know —
turn off the gurgling taps, mend leaks,
and somehow bring them back from harm
in a few days or longer weeks.

Still, death the cough persists
and life, the bravest childlike cry,
though time's still a-scalpelling,
will always ask a young and solemn 'why?'

MARY PARKER

Eiffel Tower

We had entered here and paid to press the proper buttons
mother and daughter squashed together into such small space
that seemed to get smaller and smaller
tighter and more pointed the higher up we went
but never was this to be expected—
this quite suffocating tenderness
for another person's dilemma; forget my own.
Way, way up on such a flimsy floor
with Paris spinning beneath us
and our heads sharpened to the point of a rocket
that was going to burst through the girders,
we were headed for the day-time stars in unknown skies
and would be ripped out of our bodies —
a nakedness too raw to bear.
She sank to the floor. I murmured platitudes.
We had been trying to adjust all week:
        trying to right the wrongs
avert the wrath of generations, but here was something else
almost a reverse birth-process; but what?
What could this teach us
where the squealing bats beat home to roost? — And she?
She should not be captive here with me. It was my doing.
She begged me at the summit
not to go out with the laughing crowd on to the viewing-balcony.
So I complied. I stayed with her.
        She allowed me then to stroke her hair.

LINDA ROSE PARKES

We Start Here

I love the way your chest hollows under your dressing gown;
the hair like grass on still dunes.

How when you look at me there's a dance brewing
as if Ry Cooder's on the terrace in a white suit and black shirt.

When I slipped on the wet tiles you came running, your heart on the verge
of a kaleidoscope storm ...

What if I asked you, three times a day, to shake off sloth, shake up the interior,
roll back the carpet to the hills, the river in its unhurried flow.

Or if I said: *put your hand on the beginning of the world*
and I'll put mine on the seat of contradictions

when you're drinking coffee from your yellow cup? Your cigarette papers
on the cloth, your red lighter; behind you a vase of white lilies.

Little by little, all at once we fold back the skin and show where to travel,
where to assert and lay lightly.

If I could say *here and here and here* is where your tongue
should hover, your thoughts glide to the edge

of the planet as if we were star gazing, as if we were trying to judge
the distance of a leap

between stars...
a good place to start would be the table with the cups, the lilies.

Our Father's Genitals

Two china geese on the tiled wall
flying to somewhere like far off Ottawa
or one of the Great Lakes of skittering
reeds where a hand would pass like shade
over the surface. A good sort of hand
for ruffling a wing, like the hand of our
father in gentler mood, plenty of hot water
and a glass of sherry. Him lying there
soothed inside himself; the pine's silt
needles scratching the window.
My sister and me perched on the bath,
stealing glances. Such a pale sort
of thing, full of secrets.
Surely it wanted to tell us something
in a voice that was beckoning
under the water with whispers around it.
I imagined a wily song, an ocean
of living things, pulled by currents,
remembering tides.
To think it had held one half of us
suspended like geese in mid-flight;
we might never have arrived in our blue
feathers: imagine us frozen there —
the place of shadows we had to cross
to be scooped up, wrapped in our mother.
Tentacle, sacks and limpid spine,
water lapping the rough hairs.

Intruder

Don't you ever tire of fright,
long to make light bounce at the door?
It's not easy to make dark hang back
in service to the good dream:
you have to learn to orchestrate.

Try offering him a gin and orange,
sit him in a chair under the moon
with an endless sigh of silk cushions:
he turns out to be ill-fated, young:
has left his life's work in the boot
and can't remember where he's left the car
in a warren the size of the Atlantic.
Don't let the glass shake or he'll leave
before we finish the story
which we'll call from now on:
A Fable On The Production Of Light.

It's well past midnight
when he triggers the sensors.
You've been waiting a long time
for the rasp of the door, lain there
listening, bracing yourself
to slip from your bed onto the landing,
trying to haul out your voice.
Slow motion, text-book stuff:
you still fumbling for the switch
knowing he's climbed the first stair.

PERSE PEETT

On Reading Dylan Thomas in the Pub

The Big Match: The Prince Albert is
swept by an enematic sigh
as the home team barely
fails to score. Juke-box
belting out its tunes. To right
and left loud beery
conversation, clouds of smoke.

In the midst of it all,
me and Dylan Thomas (plus Guinness).
Gripping the book, bracing my feet,
headlong into reading. White-
water rafting on a finely tuned torrent
of words, spray mist of deliberately
disintegrating imagery . . . . .
What other poet's words would
withstand such a barrage of distraction?

This *is* the way to read him.
I feel as though I could
leap up
declaim the poem
and the whole bar will
shoot their fists into the air
and roar
'YYYEEEEESSSSSS!'
then
'Eh?'
before continuing as though
nothing unusual had happened.

JEAN PESTELL

One Old Man

One old man
still
on the esplanade.
A full life,
huddled in a thin blanket.
Distant dreams,
warmer than his fraying coat.

A light breeze
coaxes open his sad eyes,
dries unshed tears.

Alone,
sounds within people his being.
Memories,
real as the gentle hand on his shoulder:
'Time to go back, dear.'

MARIO PETRUCCI

Balance
Cassino, Italy

Nonno — remember that night
you led me right up the garden
to that deckle edge of meadow,
the distant bulb dim as moonlight.
Look, you said. The field
was black. Beyond, black water.
You raised both hands, embraced
an invisible horizon.
On one side, us —

                       on the other,
Her. You think your life
is yours? Your curved finger
jabbed at earth. *No more cousins*
than She allows. She gives,
She takes. You slit your throat
with a thumbnail. *The earth.*
When I am gone who will bury
their hands in Her?

This Is Lust To Say
a Spellcheck poem

I have eaten
the plumes
hats were on
the vice box

and which
you de reprobate
waving
for breast fast

Cor give me
Hey we're delicious
so old
and so sweaty

214

Bomb

Monte Cassino, February 1944

Tip sunk in stone   I
sizzle half in   half in
Imperative

to shatter bone   Not
lodge in this bloodless
crack of Benedict's

tomb   Still I am
a fever to touch   my full
charge packed hard

Cram of fulminate
I did not happen
by accident

Now trembling hands
must engage me —
that pliers' final

snip make my striker
unable
or ram my innards

Out   casing a gasp —
Damn that gymslip
first day on

fuses who fudged
my connection
dreaming Marlene

Me — I'm awake
Need only a nudge
a hip's

vibration   The skip
of a heart-beat
is all

I take

PETER PHILLIPS

Spanish Sighs

There's a sigh hanging over the mountain.
I can hear its breath,
and if I look along the ridge
where horizon meets rock,
there it rests, languid, almost hypnotic
and because I've never seen
a sigh before, all I want to do is look.

I've felt many creep up on me,
linger in my chest,
then felt a … swoosh as they undulate
past my larynx, out into the world.
But this is different.
My eyes cling to the top of the mountain,
all craggy with trees.
It's as if the sigh is pleased
to be released in this place.

Perhaps this is where all sighs go —
our troubles and contentments,
to the top of Spanish mountains to vaporise.

Then in the time it takes me
to wonder at the taste of bougainvillea,
the sigh drifts off,
just glides away into the sky,
leaves me to stare,
slightly open mouthed.

Menorah

The seven branches of the candelabrum
have withered;
the tarnished silver no longer sparkles.

Under its base I turn the key,
once again hear
the tune played at Chanukah.

It surprises me how that tinkabell sound,
not heard since the death of my first wife,
still makes the silver sparkle.

Worried

I have a lot in my head.
This is not unusual.

My wife tells me,
I mustn't think,
and if I must
I should think about fields,
naked women, champagne and bubble bath.

I think this is incredibly nice of her.

PHIL POOLE

A Moment's Pause

That moment creeps up like a cat.
Then the moment it sniffs the air
will it settle or limber on
gifting its presence elsewhere

or arch its back smelling a rat
electrostat me with its fur
lick my cheek with the wet rasp
of its tongue, settle on my lap and purr?

I must lack fright because I must
not be the cause of its moving where
I cannot get a grasp on black
night, black cat. Is that you there?

Below The Radar Screen

On the meadow of Faith sat a hare.
Absolutely no-one should have seen them there.
Besides it was night.
On the hill of Doubt something registered
As a faint trace in the infra-red.
A moment then out of sight.

My real self, a smaller furry animal,
Knows safety in shadows
But when it feels secure
Will take a delicate *aventure,*
A stroll in the light,
There to sun itself a while,
Preen, stretch limbs, clean whiskers,
Until it feels strange eyes upon it,
Then instantly it scuttles off to hide.
I wait. It can't avoid another escapade.

HILARY PORTER

Dare Devils
Olu Deniz, Turkey

They fly and swoop
fatally attracted to
the dancing light
bright bouncing blue,
they skim, think
they can swim;
then float lifeless.
Tomorrow the man
with the net will scoop
the bodies from the pool.

They swoop and fly,
can not resist the challenge
of the sky, soar across the bay
more numerous than birds.
The bravest twists and drops
into the turquoise sea, till
the man in the boat
scoops him from the ocean.

Danger seduces moths and men alike.

Bride

Like a chrysalis she reclined;
the dream seemed lucid at the time —
seventeen, untouched by love,
he seemed to hover just above her mind.

She raised her troubled head and said
'You're welcome to my icy bed, where
I am forced to lie alone in silken sheets
as cold and dark as stone'

Though she would gladly have him stay,
he paused awhile, then turned away
returning to the night from which he came.
The merest shadow in the blind —
a product of her dormant mind?
Vanished, and he hadn't left his name.

Each night she flung the windows wide
till darkness brought him to her side ...
Silence — save the rustling of the tree.
The moment that she closed her eyes
he said *'I've come to rescue you*
from your virginity, come, lie with me'

Offering her virgin neck,
a fleeting smile (just for effect)
she tried to draw him deep into her womb;
and yet she knew each time he came, softly
whispering her name, he'd take
more of her life-blood to his tomb.

No-one can reach her now;
his face appears each night
through fluttering lace —
the curtains part to freeze her heart
in the ice of his embrace ...

The last time that he came to her
he said *'I've come to rescue you*
from your mortality, come,
fly with me' and in that moment
she became his bride.

Doorstep Cats

The doorstep cats of number 33
are many and varied.

Growing in numbers
(word has got around)
they watch from walls

and bushes and roofs; and wait—
till the merest chink
of china on stone heralds a feast,

and then as if from nowhere
they ascend the steps in their droves,
and always at the front of the queue

the old tom, scarred and ugly
commands respect from lesser cats
and stands his ground.

They scatter as I approach,
(except for Old Tom)
leaving their ambience behind.

On The Edge

The edge beckons
again and again:
tentative feet are drawn
ever closer.

Surging waves break over
rocks below; the timeless rhythms
reach my ears like a siren's song.

In the presence of *Old Harry*
my craven self yields to
a braver soul who dares

to traverse this strip of path
and reach the very pinnacle
while seagulls shriek their challenge ...

pausing to savour
this exquisite trepidation
I know I am in control —

stepping back from danger
I retrace my steps to the safety
of firmer ground

still wondering how it would have felt
to take to the skies and fly...

'Old Harry' is a rock formation off the coast of Swanage in Dorset.

FRANCES PRESLEY

24 / 4

in the ward of Aldgate
where no one lives
especially the common councilmen

a common workman said:
Go back to Bishopsgate
turn right
and you'll find it

what's left of it

a narrow space between buildings
scaffolding, mud and sca

                         folding
yellow clay on my red shoes
washed away across the pavement
falling over bollards and pipes

Get out of the way
you're making the place untidy
a foreman said to the other

Underwriters
of intimate scale
it is under written
as she found her way to the Bar

two bombs caused
great
                             dam
         age

commissioned by the worshipful company
of longbows a window
in memoriam
famous

                                 vic

            tories

Crecy, Poitiers and Agincourt

she felt the ideas could
be taken further
in contemporary glass
the bow treated in an abstract
manner yew leaves and the long curve
grows and moves
bows lend themselves
to rescue
yew leaves and the long curve

                                  the

                                       long

                                            curve

                                                yew

                                         leaves

                                   yew

cut

Ground 0

Prone veering
Bell sign
Enters Fuji
Bell sing

Grasp maws
Programmed claws
Dance over pyr ric

Features focused
Eye tongues
Prest glass
Dance over lights

Less than thin
Steps away
Test bed
Of
Filed
Filings

Be a part of it
I want to

Blow your horn
Fit the battle of

Sally sally sally's army
Find us now and at the hour

Skies over
Heavens over
Fuji

Arterial tree
Gird her soft toys

Calm/
Ing piano
Issime

JEREMY REED

Elegy For David Gascoyne

Three streets away from where I write,
plane leaves wallpaper Tanza Rd,
their floppy, star-shaped autumn mush
mashed orange round your old front door —
your 1930s sanctuary,
a base from which to walk all night

across the city's meshed network,
its bridges and financial grid
appearing almost visionary:
you hungry, drugged, and looking out
for the dawn's first campari blast
to colour red over Southwark.

Your walks to me are legendary,
deep night as a complicitous state
to constellating metaphor;
the poem memorized as hot,
then worked on by those molecules
which are its individual chemistry.

Bartok and Berg were your thrashed mix
of soundscape geometries, hit hard
into your fine-tuned, shot-down nerves.
You rose at noon, wore pinstripe suits,
a studied tie, saw London burn
in a heat-flashed, war-time apocalypse.

So often, David, I still meet
your benefactor from the time;
her speedwell-blue eyes, blue like yours,
with recollection, while we talk
through leaf-fall, with its mosaic
mottling the toad-spotted wet street.

Today, with sunlight bottled into haze
like colour in an ice-lolly,
I stand on Kite Hill and map out

the city's rudiments — your beat —
a gold star on Canary Wharf
sighting above the compact maze.

My memories of you are late,
your 1980s rediscovery;
we sharing readings, you benign
and anecdotal, telling me Breton
wrote in green ink, Crevel violet,
with total recall at the Tate.

You checked your watch compulsively
for an appointment neither made
nor kept, a secret rendezvous
with time itself, outside de Chirico's
station, framed by a dark green sky
dissolving boundaries of reality?

You gave your life to poetry,
demanding nothing, went insane
like Hölderlin, your gift burnt out,
and revisioned with dignity
the art of silence, made of it
a sort of abstract creativity.

Poets are born to give and not receive,
the story of our damaged lives
in making out: you sold your books,
your everything, no back-up then
as now, just a fraternity
attempting somehow to survive.

Breton you agreed was the last
to raise a cosh for poetry
as revolutionary credo.
Expelled from the group, you remained,
post-ECT, its survivor,
an undercover surrealist.

Your letters, I have 63,
punctuated reclusive years,
your blanks in time, no impetus
to get back, just your memories
tuned to past highlights, showing like a film
in which you were the commentary.

You are a legend to the few
who know your journey, and I feel
your presence in the smoky air,
the youthful poet, red bussing
to the West End, and Zwemmer's Books,
sometime in 1942?

I write this in a small café
you would have used at South End Green,
aware this poem's our last meeting place,
a point of contact I sustain
no matter unilaterally
throughout much of the foggy day.

You would, like me, in going back
have climbed the hill by slow degrees
and heard the Thameslink train address
the neighbourhood, and deep in thought
have pondered on the swimming leaves,
the red, the yellow and the black.

ROBERTO RIVERA-REYES

Translated by Dinah Livingstone

The Trees Sing Like Rivers

This is the story of the trees
that sing like rivers.
Air flutters in petals and leaves,
which beat by night in hundreds of hearts.
Like crystal bells
they chime down our foreheads
a night-dew of stars
that bathes our faces
in most beautiful joy.
Thus they bless the worldly talent
of constellations, planets and people
who also dance like trees
and whirl like dervishes encountering Avatar.
For trees are the joy of the city,
streets and avenues become green cathedrals
breathing at night in your dreams.
Then the planet's most urban region
grows into Amazonia.
A global lungful of air,
a whirlwind of ecstasy
and the serenity of Segismundo.
This is the story of the trees
that sing like rivers
in the dance of the planets.
Ideas, thoughts, wafting breezes
seem to be swallowed in darkness,
leaving a luminous trail.
They are my kisses swathed in eagerness
that touch your lips with emotion.
They continue their journey without us
to where love is more
than a universe expanding.

JO ROACH

Ghost In The Machine

Jack Davis in overalls, wearing a cap
after his day job as a brickie, repairs
secondhand bikes, to earn extra
to pay the mortgage on the house he painted
green white and yellow, at the time of ads
in corner shops, 'Rooms to let, no blacks no irish'.
In the box room of number sixteen, spare wheels
hang from six inch nails, the floor a shingle
of nuts and bolts, the smell of three-in-one oil
heavy as khaki. Hands fretted from wire wool
he polishes aluminium rims to silver, removes
links from the chain until it fits. His memory
full of the sea fine tunes into each wave
as if it were the one that broke when he left
a country where there are no words for yes and no.
Sue Sue Lambert shopping in Dun Laoghaire
meets one of the Davises and asks,
'Is Jack not after coming home?'

Ridley Road

Elsie shops the jostling length of Saturday bustle
cream cheese, smoked salmon, 24 hour bagel bakery,
where Mosley rallied fascists in the thirties.
Silks for saris, emerald green bridal red, patchouli incense
smells of hippy days and flower power.
Flat rounds of Turkish bread dotted with shiny black olives
waiting for feta cheese.

Clouds by the yard of Persil-white net curtains,
wide brimmed, lace trimmed, church going hats.
Sweet potato, saltfish fritters, yam, green bananas
in wooden crates stamped West Indies.
Squid are holidays eating calamares on the Costa del Sol.
A scoop full of bursting purple plums
C'm on mum, going cheap,
a row of upside-down white halal chickens.

Elsie eighteen again, would be one of the girls with figures
in lycra strides, earrings big as saucers,
mouths full of laughter, blowing a week's wages
on a sexy number to wear that night.
Frilly scanties, outsize women's,
china seconds, polished apple pyramids
punnets of strawberries, *don't squeeze the avocados,*
sugar-smelling deep-fried doughnuts,
sizzling hamburgers — *onions with it?*
megaphones blasting *Jesus loves you,*
yellow bananas hanging on hooks,
pairs of smoky kippers,
bloaters on ice, eyeballs staring
mouths wide open.

Mind yer backs trolley of boxes
pushing through Socialist Workers selling headlines.
Fly-pitching suitcases, Chanel Number 5, made in Basildon
You won't buy better   Three for a fiver   Spice girls tee shirts
Record shop singing *Hot Hot Hot*
Elsie's hips give a wiggle.

Arusha

The market not so far
even with a belly aching
it not so far. Some days
the water heavy, but that is so.
Soon I bring back cotton
from the market near Arusha
for the child my daughter
carry in her belly.
Carrying a child not so hard
as carrying the water.
Soon her waters break.
If it a girl, I teach her
how to carry, then
where to sell the water.

When I old bones
too old to carry
my daughters with strong backs
will carry to the market,
to the market near Arusha.

My Daughter

has the key to the door
no past in her eyes,

a butterfly in ankle socks
and Alice bands,

an hour is as long
as she feels,

her favourite day is
the day after tomorrow,

bums and farts make her laugh,
money is Kit-Kats and crisps,

guinea pigs are skinny pigs,
the weather can be froggy.

I hold her adult hand
to cross the road.

ANNA ROBINSON

What The Water Gave Anna

I'm lying where I washed up
a few moments ago
on the river police pier.

I'm breathing so gently
they don't seem to see
how alive I am,

how the light shines
through, as if my skin
were a lantern.

They've done all the tests,
checked my pulse,
held a feather to my nose,

now they're taking fingerprints,
checking dental records,
trying to put a name to me;

but no name can match
this seaweed tiara
and duckweed shoes —

these liquid breaths.
No name can make me
live less lightly.

Night Stick Fracture

At the museum, in the medieval
section, the bones lie tagged and boxed.
The Curator is present as always.
He begins. *Skeleton (SK 409)*

*is practically complete, the bones
are solid and well preserved.* Long stripped,

the arms lie separate. I ask,
and yes, I am allowed to touch.

This man was my age
and though tall, had rotten teeth.
His legs show he was a horseman
but I am holding his arms.

They do not crumble.
Each is as light as a drum stick
and even though they don't look like they'd be
they're smooth under my fingers.

Actually, these are
his lower arms, laid out for the grave.
The left ulna is in two
but the rest are whole.

Look says The Curator
at the mid shafts and sure
enough, each is marked with a fine
line of healing, a bone scar

and if you trace it
from the broken line of the left,
across both arms, you will have drawn
an arrow-tip as I have done.

Now, it's May Day
and we're somewhere else and there's
this boy… *No,* says The Curator, *he too
is a man, look at that fusion*

and the length of those arms
and *yes,* I say, *sorry, he looks so slight
standing there, arms crossed above his head,
as riot police slam into him.*

And you, what's happening to you?
Does your body become rigid, as you clutch

your banner poles? Or are you, like me,
a Cassandra-child who shrieks

what their helmeted ears can't hear?
Or do you face them dressed only in cotton,
a placard stick against their batons?
And is it Seattle, Paris or London?

The Curator keeps all the measurements
but he cannot tell us how to be — just
that our bare arms shame them
that our bare arms tell the tale.

The Gate Keeper

I think I woke;
at least, I think I'd been asleep,
when the gate keeper came.

I got busy;
collecting up bones, shaking mud
from my flesh, as was expected.

After, I sat
beneath the lilac, breathing it, chewing
the leaves, refreshing my breath,

holding my bundle
of body and the plumb-bob which dangled
from my hand. He watched.

The gate-keeper
doesn't speak. He never said.
It was someone else's voice

that warned me —
keep the plumb-bob straight; I flinched,
dropped everything.

I began again;
collecting up bones, shaking mud
from my flesh, as was expected.

Days Like This...

We're running, heads thrown back so we can see
how fast we are, faster than the clouds
(today's windy) and faster than the police
whose cordon we broke through at Waterloo.

There's so many of us and the sun is hanging
so low above York Road — and is bouncing itself
off so many windows it has made a long
gold tunnel that none of us could resist.

I have the megaphone — this is not normal —
I'm usually the one with the banner,
wind-surfing to rallies with some-one smaller
than me, but not today, today I can see

my long voice spreading out in front
shimmering like a heat haze towards
the bridge where it blends with others
and we look like one, we believe we can fly.

We're heading for Westminster Bridge and later,
after the stand-off and riot (which will begin
when some drift home and the crowd gets smaller
and we're stuck and night's wet-blanket takes

the shine off our skins, just before that woman
from Tottenham — Maria, I think— has her leg
broken by a police horse) will it prove
worth it? We won't get to win this one,

but we ran, heads back, down that road and now
on days like this, in a certain light, I'm weightless.

TOM RUBENS

St. Paul's

1.

First sight of the dome
Is the blue-grey curve
Summiting the ellipse
Whose slow stone-plunge
Is as yet concealed by buttresses.
At curve's top, a golden stem
Rises into the blue, glistening.

2.

From this, the eye lowers to
The deft foliage of the buttress edges,
Then down darkened lengths of latticed window,
Past wall-alcoves concavely smooth.

3.

A turn to the left through
               the churchyard gardens
Brings now a full view of the dome
               and cross,
Parabola-massive above a ring of columns,
Heavy as a hillock, yet somehow
Made light by perfect geometry;
Threshed by this morning's wind
As by that of many thousands;
Filling the same place it did
    three centuries ago.

4.

After the dome, the cathedral front:
Two high tiers of columns
Crowned with acanthus leaves, the upper
Supporting a triangular frieze
That patterns eloquence of limb.

Behind the lower tier,
In semi-shadow, stands an oblong
Door of oak in panelled squares,
Past twenty feet high, and curiously
Inducing pause, as if not all
                    were meant to enter.
Above the door are wall-figures
Contoured by folds of robes.
Here, one feels, is complexity
Of many facets, balanced, resolved,
— In whose stone-shimmer of
                    wrought proportion
One's own, not yet resolved, may rest.

    5.

The eye imbibes again
The building's august grammar
Of design, its sweeping symmetries;
Then, on a side-wall, spots
The small face of a boy.
The features are fattish, pre-pubescent,
And would not betoken strength,
Did not the lips push outward
In steady, continuous blowing,
And so link with the trumpets
                    garlanding the head.
The realisation comes that
In this exhaling lies the power
To raise cathedrals, to infuse
Conception and the will to forge.
This face, perhaps, is Wren's appended
Signature to his all-stilling work.

MYRA SCHNEIDER

Amazon

for Grevel

For four months
all those Matisse and Picasso women
draped against
plants, balconies, Mediterranean sea, skies
have taunted me
with the beautiful globes of their breasts as I've filled

my emptiness
with pages of scrawl, with fecund May, its floods
of green, its irrepressible
wedding-lace white, buttercup gold,
but failed to cover
the image of myself as a misshapen clown

until you reminded me
that in Greek myth the most revered women
were the single-breasted
Amazons who mastered javelins, bows, rode
horses into battle,
whose fierce queens were renowned for their femininity.

Then recognising the fields I'd fought my way across
I raised my shield
of glistening words, saw it echoed the sun.

The Orange Trees Of Seville

I step from a taxi to a scent that hints
tropical heat, to the glass shine
of doors opening to other lives.
And it's real — the perfume piercing
the air is everywhere, its source
the blossom in small white marriages
on trees nested with globes, each
so orange it carries the red tinge
of a huge moon slung low in the sky.

The trees stand in pairs sweetening
avenue, square, passageway.
And at the centre of old courtyards,
whose Moorish arches lead to rooms
silken with darkness, I come upon them
standing in epiphanies of light
as if they never shed rubbery leaves,
ecstatic blossom, as if their oranges
are the perpetual I'm continually trying
to cup in my hands without questioning
whether *always* is a prize I want.

Piano

after 'La petite pianiste, robe bleue, fond rouge' by Henri Matisse

So enticing: her baby blue dress,
its wide collar, her marriage
to the piano dressed in a foxy red
and sienna body, the glide

of her hands over its white teeth.
So beguiling the open pages,
their notes fantasies that echo the wild
dance of bouquets in the gold

arches painted on the coral wallpaper.
He's made her the focal point:
a skyblue body with damson clefts
and holding out sticks that drift

into the keys, a craning neck stem
whose bloom is a pale blob
capped by brown and notched with a bead
eye. He's not interested in the seed

of self at her core. If she's longing
to become someone she must
unstiffen those gawky arms, muster
her rounded shoulders, fluster

the ferny pot plant, her meekly
tucked hair, the pages
of scored music and, throwing a stone
at the piano, compose her own.

GAVIN SELERIE

Jackety Jiggit

When you know the answer you still forget.

What is the secret of the Green Chamber?
Where is the deed in the red box?
How do you move behind stamped leather?
Which is the flower that reduces space?
Why speak French from a spire of hair?
Whose is the face resurrected?

Is there a devil in Deverell?
Suspicions are one thing, certainties another.

Many-fold Festo

The **part** brought *in*
threatens
to explode
the **whole**

the whole

is *Only*
the **holding**
coOrDiNaJes

BILL SHERMAN

To End With A Thought From Thomas Wyatt

he awakens from another dream of shattered love
recalling how he wrote the words which no one understands
least of all himself. and so he tears the paper scraps
and sees them safely through the gutter grate.

and when that rhythm breaks, all maps do change.
the long declining hills of Devonshire he used to walk
become the alien city, the locked doors of his own spirit
cramped in a land of too many dreaming Caesars:
the impossible shadow-play of love.   he awakens.

he himself betrayer of dreams and loves —
in the house of death and witchcraft, there is an old film
he has yet to see.   but he is tired
and wants them all, the gaggle of surrounding lovers lost,
to disappear.   and so they do, to reappear in dream —

the *nouvelle vague* of his mind.   & she is there.   & she.   & she.
and these women whom he has loved and lost
return as wispy visions to which he clings
as others he thought friends do rail at him.

The Storehouse Of Imperialist Theft

The British Museum with the support of Government continues to
withstand demands for the return of parts of its collections —
(from the statement of the Board of Trustees of the British Museum, 1999)

Not happy that Tiki from Rurutu
    No sunshine in the BM
        He needs to go home

You'd oppose cruelty to humans
    Cruelty to animals
        Bad *mana* the London Missionary Society

Bringing that Tiki with them

Woe to they took it away

John Williams, 1821,
　　18 years later
　　　　he is eaten in Melanesia
　　　　　　Coconut radio got word out
　　　　　　　　— thieves about

Bligh no better, could have sailed to Tubuai
　　a few hundred miles
　　　　told his men in the boat
　　　　they are cannibal

to make his journey
　　Not true — Tubuai
　　not a cannibal island

& Cook, his mind went
　　& he started killing Polynesians

What did he do, anyway
　　Moa Tetua's ancestors
　　　　did not, we

without sextant nor compass —
　　only the stars
　　　　the swells
　　　　　　the clouds
　　　　　　　　the birds

mana – *Tahitian for spiritual power*
Moa Tetua – *Foremost Tahitian poet of the 19th century, he was both blind and
a sufferer from Hansen's Disease. Four of his* rari *(love chants) were translated
by Samuel Elbert and Muriel Rukeyser.*

243

Soft Samoan Night

women wear their flowers here
   opposite to Tahitian
      significations

the pretty young hotel desk clerk
   said

& here
   they think Savaii
      is the place
         from where
            the long journeys
              began
not Raiatea

last hours in a place
   one does not expect to return to
      always fills the soul with sadness

or is it not 'soul'
   so much as being alone
      without a woman
         to take me home

best not to talk
   to Polynesian women —
      it only makes me lonely later

causes me to write
   & who needs
      introverted libido flow
         to lessen anxiety

that's three 'me'
   in 3 stanzas
      4
         if you count this one

all useless failure
   neurotic death-orientated drivel

      an old lone wolf
   not wanting to be one
      grows older

LABI SIFFRE

suspended affirmation

today i exchanged my raven for a multi-coloured parrot
my black limousine for a two wheeled wooden cart
and a donkey with pink painted hooves and a straw hat
with holes for his earringed ears, my CD collection
of Gregorian Chants for Samba, Salsa, High Life
the complete works of Barry White and of course
Sexual Healing by Marvin Gaye

today i exchanged my thursday bridge nights with Mrs Ogilvy
her husband, his malodorous pipe and the village
eccentric, Lavinia DeVentre, for regular visits to the *Death
by Rollercoaster* and *Candy Floss Park*

today i exchanged my Man of Means weeds for cut off jeans
and Hawaiian shirts, my Oxford brogues for bare feet
my cultivated air of detachment for a permanent silly smile
the wine bar for walks in the forest, the golf club lounge
for the Snug in 'The Three Legged Dog', afternoons
in galleries of contemporary art for pinball machines
a comfortable sex life for almost permanently blue balls
my work is my life for my life is yours

today i exchanged
my raven for a multi-coloured parrot
last night we made love nine times
Yes   Nine Times

today   i still don't know how *you* feel

let's dance

in the
 chemical warfare and
                weapons
     of mass destruction
              department
   of a Catalonian supermarket
          i learned la cucaracha
               is the cockroach

      that hardy and persistent creature
     tolerant both of microwave and nuclear
    radiation made its way to world domination
  millions of years before we humans came to play

           and when
       in a final solution worthy of our rationality
     allergy   we end our charade (as masters
    of the universe under a god we made
      in practice merely to evade)
          then
          with the moonlight melting
       in a spiral of sky
               mid an infinite indifference
          of wherefores ways and why
  the king and queen of cockroaches
          to their children's loving gaze
     will, with delicacy and gravitas,
                          dance
               la cucaracha
               on our
      suitably shallow
      mass grave

the good guys

i have a monkey on a string
he does not sing and he does not grin
he chatters out of nervousness and rage
he bears his teeth in a threatening
i write his life with lies i call historicling
no matter what he cannot win

i have a monkey on a string
he climbs so high almost reaches
my chin and when he reaches to the top
i let him drop no matter that he wants
to stay i rest assured *i* rule his day

i have a monkey on a string
last night he tried to kill me
with a safety pin
i took the poker from the fire
and with a flourish ended him
entire

DENNIS SIMMONS

Anti-Biotical

It's stopped the 'flem'
already
but I've got a voice
like a back door groaning.

I'll have the flu-jab
next year
just to stop having to take
these awful tablets.

I can see what they
mean
no corn flakes, etc.
—there's enough iron
in me
for an old rusty tool
from my Father's
cellar

Still coughing for the moment
and *what* a horrible taste
in my mouth—
mind you —
it *was* bad before too,
just different

I feel I want to take my hate out
on something, as a punch-bag
Bang, bang
Take That! Doctor
Crash, smash
Take That! medicine
TAKE THAT!
LIFE

JANET SIMON

Over The Top

Sweet Jesus, look up
at that evening sky.
What colour is it —
exactly?
Cobalt of turquoise?
Prussian-marine?
Royal-gentian
with underlays of green?
It's like the livid skin
of some half fallen angel,
bruised for the sake of beauty.

I want to kneel down
like a little child
and pray under that canvas.
I want to stretch up high
beyond my adult years
and lick its indescribability.

I could prostrate myself
and drown under the subtle
layer upon layer silence
of its plunging blues.
I could stand up, reach out
and smack one hand against
its louder, flatter planes.

I want to hear the sound
of its applause.
It has the shade of rivers,
seas and flowers all together.
I want to smell its sunless glory.
I want to swallow
all its depth and surface.

Right here above my head
is the penultimate.

That precise spot,
this everywhere
which keeps pace with me
as I struggle home,
haloes my ground.
It quickens my tired legs,
prizes my lips apart
and wets my tight, dry tongue
with spit enough to call it names.

Barely articulate, almost struck dumb
by what escapes my powers of definition,
I come with violent, sweet blasphemies
of love to shout at you.

O God. O Christ.
O evening sky.
O fucking miracle.

King Harvest (has surely come?)

Pity he has, of course, for the poor... but Christ has far more pity for the rich, for the hard hedonist, for those who waste their freedom in becoming slaves to things. — Oscar Wilde (De Profundis)

I waited for you
by the ornamental bridge.
You did not come.
The roses were fading
on the cusp of summer and autumn.
The air was turning.
I felt its suggestion of bite,
its promise of ripe achievement.
If you come in winter
I will not turn you away.

I miss your pale, smooth body,
your educated vowels,
your blithe pornography,
your love of money.

The nights grow harder.
The homeless come to me.
I ring the hostels.
They have no room.
You do not come
and my imagination fails me.
It hurts to send men
out onto the streets.
I lack resources.
Perhaps tomorrow
I will do more for them.

Perhaps also, you will cross over
to see me in the next month or so,
when leaves become the colour
of glowing embers.
You may still be as captive
as you were before,
but I will have the freedom
to warm your blood a little
when the cold weather shelters open,
and I can offer you
some small, fat respite
until the spring.

Stone

You would reduce this stone to something homely.
Set in the palm of your soft hand,
it rests as if it wouldn't harm a fly.
In your pink fingers, it is a generous stone.
You offer its smooth surface as the best
of possibilities in the best possible of worlds.

> You pass this stone to me
> with pleasing manners.
> You sanction me to hold it
> for a few minutes
> and to speak uninterrupted
> in my own defence.

Your gracious patronage
reduces me to gibberish.
To avoid stuttering
I place this outsized pebble
in my quivering mouth.

Its frigid texture
is cold, impenetrable.
I cannot chew on it
I spit it out.

An angry passer-by
picks up this stone
and hurls it
through your window.
Your creamy skin
turns puce-vermilion,
and as he runs away,
you bolt your doors
and ring for the police.

I bend down and pick up
this stone.
It hasn't changed
its shape or colour.
Its unrelenting stoneness
pleads with me.

I do not understand what force of hatred
makes a man destroy your house,
what speed of terror grabs you to defend it,
but I accept this stone. I hear its silent plea
of guiltless being. It sings to me
in my own ignorance, 'I am a stone.'
And a stone is a stone is a stone is a stone

HYLDA SIMS

The Bass Player & The Band Leader's Wife

You played the bass, you were just seventeen
and talented; your hair, your eyelashes
were pale and long, they swept me off my feet
and turned my legs to quavers; we were rash
as well as wrong but it was such a passion
we had no sense to spare. You spread your coat
on stony ground behind the Ritzy: the splash
of rain, lights from the street, we seem to float
as if that old bomb site were sea and we were boat

and in our slipstream what'd been solid ground
was maelstrom, nothing that was built could stand
my life was lost, my loved ones nearly drowned.
We two were washed on separate spits of land
in separate oceans, you joined a touring band
whilst I, clutching to wrack and flotsam, tried
to find my way back home. On every hand
were shipwrecks, lamps along the street beside
the flea-pit burned cold and yellow, this was winter tide…

We meet by chance, you're fifty something, you've grown
wide open, *It took me years*, you say, *I loved you
so much…* This guilt I've carried on my own
for ages lifts, becomes a ballad, two
voices reprising a song. We wear our new
faces, settled and plain, this secret scar
identifies us still, a rendezvous
deep in the shell, where the best pearls are…
All posh the Ritzy now.   *I know, three screens, a bar.*

A Measure Of Expropriation

He sprints across the back; no lights; a chill of fear;
rams the metal in the wood, yanks it, bolts the front door
breathes out and cops a look around: not much to eat
grabs an apple from a bowl, helps himself to chocolate
glancing out the window, makes some calls — long distance
shaking a bit, puts on a shirt, some Mozart, stands and listens
finds a fiver in a pot, goes for a piss
drops his jeans, ragged on the carpet, can't resist
the way they concertina on the pile, as if
the wearer melted down— something for them (the hems are stiff
with mud) a piece of art; he's no use for a suit
selects a sweater, chinos — thick, lined jacket, goes for the boots,
chooses some tapes, Ella, Clapton... hears the click
...a car door...moves...quick, out the back door...a racing bike
(he'd clocked it) tucks the chinos in, sweating— there
the broken fence... no lights, freewheels away, wind in his hair

Didn't find the gin, the bastard! he pours one, calling
the cops. His hands flex...*she must have set it...mess...appalling
...they're filth...Rolex, laptop, cameras and the rest...*
She hates the way he lies spontaneously like that, his first
instinct, something slick...*Insured, oh yeah!* his thumb
punches the phone...something slick and cold. She stares past him:
the knackered denims — insult? gift? explanation?
— and gets herself a scotch. A Little Night Music plays on

What A Miracle!

A Russian quintet busking outside Dorothy Perkins
in Ipswich, popular classics, Bizet, Gounod and good
two silver cornets, tuba, tarnished trombone and curly French horn
all their notes perfect and clean, working
so well together you don't notice the horn till you've stood
a little to pick out its shy middle tones, like the dawn

lingering and strolling under the day-breaking trumpets
over the night-hearted tuba completing the chord
Welcome from St Petersburg students, a notice says
propped on a trombone case, *Ochen Xorosho,* I murmur, crumpling
a fiver which I wonder if I can afford
then remember who I am and throw it in the case,

remember how I've always been a busker's moll
how my first lover played the violin in an arcade
below Trafalgar Square, the Bach Busker, he was a red
and Jewish and could never play at all
for a captive audience, there because they'd paid.
He felt safe only when people were led

by the ear to his unexpected delicate vibrato
behind the thrum of buses and cars,
able to stroll past or just stand there
listening to the fierce bowed chords and spiccato
deflecting from shop windows and the milk bar
on the corner into perfectly composed air.

I stand now, listening to the band
tearful, while the citizens of Ipswich
gather and pass, gather and pass...where these five lads,
whose grandparents never saw London and Amsterdam
or Ipswich and loved Joseph Stalin and Vladimir Illych
Lenin, because things had got fairer than they had

been, are now playing *When I'm Sixty-Four*
maybe for me (I've been here some time) a deep oom pah pah
from the tuba, trumpets sounding transatlantic
now, French horn quoting the counter-melody with a flare
trombone bending in some Gershwinny wah wah,
notes golden as a Kremlin dome but democratic.

Kakaya chuda! As my Russian teacher said
the day she heard they'd put a man in space.

Kakaya chuda – *what a miracle!,* Ochen Xorosho – *very good*

RUTH SMITH

Night Stop

The light's not reached us yet. When we've dozed
and dreamed once more, it will surprise us. With walls
this thin we startle easily. Behind these zip-closed
doors we cannot place ourselves at all
for we arrived here only yesterday at sundown
spotting the caravans drawn up on deep
green terraces, though we saw no-one.
The day rushed into dark. We needed sleep
and felt the hush close in all round us till
the racket broke — those fist-sized frogs trapped
in the unfilled pool rasped like a sawmill
all night long, ballooned and then collapsed
into flat silence. We'll turn and sleep again.
It's our amen to the frogs' prayer for rain.

Close Quarters

It could have been designed by Wren.
We shake it out of its bag and slot
the jointed poles that raise it
into an apse. An opening
at either end admits us
to the nylon dome that fills
with northern light or holds its heat
under the high bake of a meseta sun.

Inside its lightweight walls
we've heard the sea,
thin cries from mountain birds,
treefuls of sparrows, cracked
cathedral bells, infrequent trains,
a bullfrog all-nighter— and in the Alpujarras
once, two village clocks so out of synch
that midnight came round twice.

Each time we peg it down
to shallow-root it in another place
we disturb yesterday's dust
and shake from its folds red soil,
the blossom of olive trees, trapped
insects that have travelled here with us.
Going we leave behind, true measure
of ourselves, a double impress in the grass.

After A Hard Day At The Alhambra

In the women's showers
at *Granada Camping*
I check below door-level,
study the shift
and stir of feet,
listen for water
that splutters to a halt,
a shuffle, a pause,
the swssssh of body spray.

But I'm dreaming of pillars
and arches, walls
tiled with diamonds
and tumbling stars
where heavy steams
condense and women
in musk and sequins
henna their nails,
dab wrists with ambergris.

It's my turn now.
In the thin-walled cubicle
I find a hook
for my towelling robe,
juggle with soap
rinse out shampoo
and flip-flop back
humming the song
their blind musicians played.

EMILY TAYLOR

Her Night

It was then I needed to break
into her glass sereneness.
She is as startled as I am
that angry night.
I almost knocked through their
wooded disguise so they could bleed.
Selfishly I suppose.
Never the less, something would be true.
Why was it we walked?
To run!
So angry we the night.
We were no place under that moon.
I expected my mother's hate to find me
and die as before,
by the shelter of the open ruins
she built and knocked,
built and knocked.
Her contempt was frail.
I gave too much moon
to see that little light was thrown.
For our brief exposure
was so little to that real wind.
And the stars.
Were they too shy of the shouts
we gave and lost just for ourselves?
The blind unknowing.
Losing our hate in our arms.
That night only knows
our secrecies.

Lost Thursdays

The flowers are awake.
Some weeks older now.
They panic, I pause,
for each chilled droplet
and neither of us too surprised.
A piece of bench will be dried
when I leave.
Listening to breathless dogs
and mothers who won't listen
to the rain.
The long shapes who at present
should have left but still arrive.
I introduce myself silently.
The flowers and I most formally await.
Guards outside their stations.
At face, each damp breeze
prints a word as I shiver,
colonised by fear.
This urban dusk will not stop
for just anyone.

ALYSON TORNS

The Gate

Open the rusty red gate to the world.
Stop hiding behind the oak tree
frozen and trembling,
crying consonants,
assembling the jumble
into the needed words.

A robin sings to me
as I pluck daisies
from the soil,
cupping them in my hand.

In my mind,
my stomach,
burn memories.
Faces of friends
and loved ones
fall like flakes of ash.

Child's Play

Did anyone hear them
the dead children?
Did no one hear their cries for help?

We tied the ropes to the top bunk bed,
there was no other way out
we weren't messing around
now we are dead.

We weren't playing but hanging.

The game must have gone wrong,
their parents said. *They were playing,*
they were inseparable, loved joking around.

The newspaper said we were playing a game.
The CD kept playing
they were just kids having fun.

The Aftermath

People discarded
like forgotten sacks of rubbish.
Uprooted trees
underground despair,
old voices shrill like birds,
children gone to pastures golder.

The decaying shells of the buildings.
Black iron fire escapes still survive;
entrails erode into nothing.

Children wail and scream,
no-one listens.
People pass one another by
watching two little ladies with
red woollen hats

on their heads, handbags
clenched,
lucky to have survived.

CHRISTOPHER TRUMAN

Prague Spring 1992

Once all a very dirty beige,
the Prague trams ran advertising.

Marlboro Cigarettes
roamed the *Sudetenland,*

a cool Spring in the air.
You could see the past coming.

A girl in bright red at my bar
sipped little or no alcohol,

just juice from an orchard
laced with barbed wire.

She was cutting a new deal.
The brash guy leaning into her

was too drunk, reeled
to the floor, then a door

closed hard on him thereafter.

Insomnia, Leipzig 1982

A wind howls out of the Ukraine,
solemnising, loathed winter and summer,
as crowds tug a runway fence
imprisoned by Potsdam, the Revolution.

Crouched, green traffic police bivouac
in camouflaged tents, Saxon soldiers
by the cracking concrete nazi autobahn,
storm an accident over ridged ruts—

meeker than our *Stasi* City Control,
rotoring sleep in a food shortage.
Freighting the brown coal to save diesel,
trams, screaming, buckle their undercarriage —

perpetual, the shriek of sagging trams
run, overwrought, through the inhuman night,
shunting quieter than the Russian judder
in the helicopters circling Leipzig.

The streets are long, trapped
by the curfew's cold starvation
and the sharp echo of the peak-capped
patrols loitering the night towards you.

Awake, the hammering regime will whip
the subjugated protest of a brain
in sleep; loyalties twist
and meet the re-directed scythe.

Forming below the frieze of a façade,
ice juts on the cell glass of the torture
room in a cream tower block for the barred.
Below *'Verboten!'* a skull and crossbones.

Old histrionics peel in a light breeze
when a few leave, to go bugging black telephones.

Vilnian Breakfast, After The Coup

for Rita

In the forest, Soviet tank squadrons
charged around in circles, crushing the pine,
their engine plumes darker than ever.
They had shelled the city TV station.

Most of their gnarled-leather, Baltic stooges
had left, moved on to another camp.
A few knelt, cleaning the kitchen microphones
run to the hungry, fuggy dens of power,

the Central heating at a temperature
in mid-summer, high enough for the Arctic—
and wheezing to a civic thermostat.
The restaurant was preparing raw breakfast

for the few. *Reserved...*for men with hard currency,
proper contacts. On every Venetian blind
drawn down tight, a heavy coating of dust
by convenient grime on the street window

a summer sun could barely irradiate.
On the next-door table lay a clean revolver
from the black leather holster of a guard
eating a breakfast of sour cabbage

and jaded onions in the ochre restaurant:
he kept on angering the beady flies,
and the back of his vest grew dark with sweat.
A swing door closed, another opened quickly.

Out in a Party suburb, russet bulldozers
puffed to dig over an enviable hill,
gouge a row of immaculate cream villas
for those on the right side of a coup.

Within a month, the man I was awaiting
lay dead, a perfect bullet through the brain.

CHRISTOPHER TWIGG

Nicanor Parra

After his reading in Concepción
when crowds were thronging round him in the foyer
I waited patiently and took my chance.
'You come most carefully upon your hour'
said Nicanor in gentle English tones
and then 'Why don't you come and visit me
in Las Cruces?', he wrote his number down
on a scrap of paper which I still treasure.
I travelled to Temuco and from there
down to the coast, stayed in an old hotel,
with rattling windows and a wild sea.
I walked along the shore and turned inland
to Indian villages, men on horseback
stopped me for cigarettes, another man
was mourning for his mother who had died.
I flew to Santiago in the night.
The next day took the bus to Las Cruces
and found a room in the Hotel Trouville.
It had a kitchen with delightful views
over the beach where bathers formed a pier.
The sea was red with seaweed, thick as soup.

They showed me where he lived behind the beach
a wooden house with gardens at the front.
His maid opened the door. 'Don Christopher'.
She led me through to a small study where
I sat until Don Nicanor appeared
in white like Nehru, loosely flowing white.
I nervously shook hands. My neck was stiff,
my head ached too as if I'd grapes of lead
behind the eyes. What could we talk about?
And was I an impostor in that house?
He gently gave me confidence to speak.
I asked if he thought Whitman had a sense
of humour. *'Parece que no'* he replied,
'It seems that he did not'. It made him smile.
He told me how he'd rescued Robert Lowell
from drowning off the coast of Venezuela.

I said 'Don Nicanor please tell me if
I'm tiring you.' (For he was eighty-three).
'I'm skilled at getting rid of people who
are wearying. You'll know when I get tired'.
We drank our tea and then he opened wine
and after supper pointed out the lights
of San Antonio beyond the bay,
the *lindo puerto*, grim, industrial,
made famous in his brother's décimas.
He put on a CD. 'Listen to this'.
At first I didn't recognize the voice
as rough and black as coal from under sea
shiny and ancient too with dreams of wood
and mined in sweat by men who would not bow.
'Roberto Parra … he was always drunk
from boyhood on, just playing in the bars.
Uneducated, look at his writing.
A simple, noble soul. All that he earned
in Paris from *La Negra Ester*
he spent it all on whores…'
                              I asked to sing —
and wondered who had touched that same guitar
(we never spoke of Violeta there)
— a ballad of my father's life. He said:
'Your father was a year older than me.
I too knew Oxford, kind Port Meadow girls
for them a Chilean was most exotic.
My own father was distant. He died young.
That's why I never went for drink myself.
Come back tomorrow and we'll talk some more'.

I joined the timid bathers in the waves
before breakfast, swam in that crimson sea
where they held one another fearfully.
I watched a diver working off the rocks
who gathered crabs and crawfish in a sack.
He was alone and unapproachable.
Then I returned to Nicanor again.
He said 'Let's walk'. It must have been round six.
He led the way along the coastal road.

And now it seemed to me that Parra looked
more like a Shaman than an Indian sage
an Inca Shaman, steely, focussed, wild,
regretting *'la ferocidad perdida'*
in poetry and in mankind as well.
The town came to an end in dirty sands
where we turned back. Women came up to him.
There was a funfair, people selling food.
A student and his girlfriend tore a box
of cigarettes for Nicanor to sign.
'My friend from England he's a poet too.'
The next day was the one I had to leave.
The maid had been to San Antonio
to buy *marisco* — mussels which she steamed
and served us in a little dining room.
I asked if he would sign his book. He wrote
"for Christopher, *obispo de Londres,*
estas antigüallas del siglo XX"
(these antique lines of twentieth century verse).
We parted in the street —he held me close —
I said some words about 'an awkward bow'.
And now with tears and gladness in my heart
walked down the hill to board the waiting bus.

DUBRAVKA VELASEVIC

How We Dined

'I'd like an empty restaurant' — you said

Your wish was quickly granted —
So it was

The Romanesque medieval arches
The frescoed rooms with old stoves
The reindeer heads on the walls

'I'd like to eat caviar tonight' — you said
'*Astrakhan* on those exquisite blinis
To share the taste of Odessa
And then — that Count Stanislawski well done steak'

'And I — I'd like to listen to Chopin tonight
While I dine — where the centuries of Polish nobility
Used to dine...'

I'd like the wild boar —
The wilder the better
Tendered in wine
Chased out from the deepest forests of Poland

And before that maybe a starter —
That special crab from the shores of Russia
Sweetened by the rains — you know, Caspian

And what wine shall we drink —
Red, for sure
Like the blood roaming through the heart

And a toast
To what — shall we have?

To us
To life — bringing us together again

To this cleansing rain
In Warsaw tonight

Yes, let's drink!
And let's get drunk!

CRISTINA VITI

Multiple Frequencies

The deepening blue nuances of the flower
cut in the precious stone of a summer evening
come alive under your fingers
resonate in ethereal harmonics
in your eyes glimpsed through tears.

It is the blue that echoes
with the faraway laughter of mermaids
with the gold of Venice in spring
with the names of unknown seas
traced on a map by a child's hand.

Yes, it is that Pacific blue
enfolding a river of burning lava
to form an obsidian island where palm trees will grow
                    in distant futures
for lovers to watch the sun rise
lying side by side in hammocks of flowers.

JENNY VUGLAR

The Underwriter From Lloyds

I can feel the rain coming, the way
the wind lifts, the way the poplars whiten.

I can hold a boat upright in a storm;
twist sails in and out of wind.

I can hold four glasses and not spill a drop
though the walls close and the floor rocks.

I can see numbers like small lights
in the dark, green or white of street lamps.

I can plot the course of a wave,
watch the wind swirl without missing an equation.

I can stand anywhere, and with nothing but
fingertips, feel the rain coming.

Northland

New Zealand 9 July 1962

The last beach, pointing North,
the thin strip of land we stood upon.

The oceans were always too close for comfort.

At night I could hear the crash of seas,
where the spirits leap, see the sky open.

On a globe I traced the outline with my finger
so narrow a thick pen would obliterate us;

if I looked up, the sky was the same blue.
It was everywhere, we were drifting into it.

Rata and I crept into the porch to play knuckle bones.
We were hidden there, the light was oblique.
We played all afternoon, the same game, over and over.
Inside we could hear singing.

The day was so long we hid, crawled under the house,
hearts thumping against the floorboards.
The music here was muffled by feet tapping,
light shone thinly between the cracks.

We lay in the dust until we heard them calling,
came out and the sky was crimson red.

When I went home no one scolded. I bathed

and ate and watched the bone white stars go out.
'The sea is burning', I said and no one spoke
but all night the sky grew redder till I slept.

I dreamt of water flaming in the air,
of sea like lava, of everything there was afire.

But in the morning all there was, was blue.

Fox

The fox at the bottom of our garden stands four square,
the she wolf who fed Romulus and Remus,
dependable, looking out on danger;
coat moulting, the tilt of her head weary.
The cubs tumbling across the hellebores,
pushing to suckle, have yet to draw furrows.

Upstairs Hannah is playing a few bars on the piano,
the same bars, again and again.
Hester is reading Dogstar.
I walk from window to window, watching.

She digs deeper under the shed —
two more exits; the dust dry soil
burying the pulmonaria. Half a clay pipe
unburied today; tomorrow mosaics,
flint arrow heads, the flat bones of mastodons.

I leave her fish skins; a rabbit waits
defrosting in the kitchen.
I henna my grey hair red. Curl my tail.
The cat sniffs suspiciously at my ankles.
While the girls sleep we will sit in the moonlight,
the fox and I, waiting.

STEPHEN WATTS

Brick Lane

after the death of Altab Ali,
and for Bill Fishman

Whoever has walked slowly down Brick Lane
   in the darkening air and a stiff little
      rain,
past the curry house with lascivious frescoes,
past the casual Sylheti sweet-shops and cafés
and the Huguenot silk attics of Fournier Street,
and the mosque that before was a synagogue
   and before that a chapel,
whoever has walked down that darkening tunnel
   of rich history
from Bethnal Green to Osborne Street at Aldgate,
past the sweat-shops at night and imams with
     hennaed hair,
and recalls the beigel-sellers on the pavements,
     windows candled to Friday night,
would know this street is a seamless cloth, this
     city, these people,
and would not suffocate ever from formlessness
     or abrupted memory,
would know rich history is the present before us,
laid out like a cloth – a cloth for the wearing –
     with bits of mirror and coloured stuff,
and can walk slowly down Brick Lane from end
     to seamless end,
looped in the air and the light of it, in the human
     lattice of it, the
blood and exhausted flesh of it, and the words
     grown bright with the body's belief,
     and life to be fought for and never to be
     taken away.

Marginal Note In Time Of War

His name was not written — Hannah Arendt

Walter Benjamin took his own
life out of pure exhaustion, walking
into the mountains against love's gravity
up the scarp slope of his melting reason
to where he was abandoned by language.
Huge lethargies in the world glutted him
then stiff blood came, pulsed out in coils.
Who knows where he could have gone to
after that, except he couldn't go on, burst
by the butchered choice of angel history,
a tremendous shattering tossed across his
face, tiny maggots gobbling on sunlight,
fascisms in the honeys of his friendship.
His name unwritten, nowhere to be seen.
He who was the loveliest among people.
Why did no-one tell him when he lived?
Nothing was left to hold him on the hill.
Angels could not put back insane reason.
Exhaustion killed him, more than terror,
more than despair, or a theology of dirt.
At the end — when the angel of history
called out his name to mock him — he
walked higher up into the blind frontier
and took his own life on a hillside that
looks over the sea: one of the loveliest
places on earth, as Hannah Arendt said,
        and like himself, halfway up
        and halfway down.

A Very Little Light

Uma pequenina luz — Jorge de Sena

Simply for the breath of staying alive
        I should talk to you,
simply to pass some words across a table
                as bread or oil,
and not have them die in me. Or
                        die in you.
                And as I
measure by measure slowly toss the crisp
herbs of speech over towards your face,
a very little light will come into my eyes,
        a very little light
will glow out at you and enter your eyes
and will be returned to me and calm our
        mouths against duplicity.
And when all the bitter fratricides are
        piled up about us
this little light, this tiny flame out on the
        waste patch,
this wind-shaped tent that is your eye
        with its slow torch,
this flickered heart with its ventricles
        that beat and pump,
will provoke in us a bonfire and the will
        to live,
and even from the embers there will glow
        a little light, a very little
                shining light,
as we pass some words across the table,
        simply for the breath of
                staying alive

PVT WEST

Mission Statement

Yes, it is blood
we crave.
It is our business
to get gush, to
cut to the guts.
Vital juice
such as sap
that can ooze
too suits us.

Yes, it is blood
congealed
on our blade.
Cutlery concealed
in the drawer
of your mother's sideboard,
tangs thrust into hafts,
has cruel
edges, fatal
as a duel.

Yes, it is blood
this lust runs in. Our
forefathers flint;
gods cutlers & carvers;
near cousins swords & assegais;
distant, scissors & sharp-tined forks.

Yes, it is blood
our ambition seeks.
We slash & sever,
pare & rupture,
thrust asunder;
want to cause rivers of it
to engorge chasms
in rapture.

Yes, it is blood
that lurks in and blushes
concupiscent petals
of wound-flowers in spasm.
Before you can say *knife*
we twist in. We
plunder & plunder.
Are out for it.

BRENDA WILLIAMS

For John Horder

I watch the day distance itself over
Hampstead Heath and from an open window
Of a psychiatric ward I wonder
With the last steadfast leaves falling below
Why am I here. Were the nights as a child
With my mother and our endless journey
Through the streets of Leeds, through desperate wild
Rain just to end in vain in a room here?
While November trees hold the listless leaves
Held within the first fold of memory,
How the end of a single leaf retrieves
The meaning I have lost, how childhood's key
Is broken fast within its lock. Leaves late
In their own stillness falter as I wait.

*   *   *   *

You stand at the terminus of the one
Three nine and the shops of West End Green are
Closing round us over a reflection
From another time somewhere in a far
Place other than this where we are patients
Pausing on our way from a nearby day
Hospital and mourning both for time once
Known and the pain of time to come that lay
As an endless June rain an evening
Settling softly about us. The same age
And yet the same loss experiencing
Itself through knowledge that cannot assuage
The emptiness of unborn children or
Those who have grown and gone from the heart's core.

RAY WILLMOTT

The Walnut Gatherer

One unhavened turns his face
to us safe in our passing coach —
his shaven-headed
labourer face
sour as juice of walnuts,
bending double, level-backed
like a grounded crow,
picking up each nut one by one
from the shoe-deep mud field
day-dark with rain,
pitching it into
the little wickerwork basket,
skewed like a toppled birds nest,
seeking out the one
most cerebrum-like
in its doublings,
nub of his own lost self.

Redundant

We've got a god
who notices the fall
of every sparrow.
This capacity
is now redundant though
as the sparrows
have become extinct.

Handprints

Before there was writing
there was reading —
before there was speech
there was reading:
ancient hunters calling the game
from its tracks and traces.

Negative handprints
on the unbuilt wall
outlined in red ochre
blown fluid from the mouth.
Still by torchlight
we can read them:
so many hands
missing finger-joints,
it becomes a healing ritual —
touch the walls of the sacred cave
and fingers will grow back again.

This hand has four fingers,
that one only three.
How long must they wait
to be whole?
Meanwhile, counting is invented.

DILYS WOOD

Veronica

for Veronica Rospigliosi

First Meeting on a Writing Course in Wales

The country's rough accent
  throaty Welsh of wind and rain —
    made us talk...

Water-whips from larch
  lashed, beaded our hair,
    'Look!', bright mops, spangled

like moss, and moss
  tressed down, long falls
    of weightless green,

and your voice
  made music like rain,
    rain like your voice —

threads, words traced down
  making a pure
    clarified pool.

Woman in the Moon — the 1999 Eclipse

On screen, eclipse, as cancer
  eclipses you and we

dare not watch — let the TV
  (blue moon on gold) image

a thin white face, *cameo*
  of a dead friend. But you're tough,

want a warm wrap, please — this year's
  pashmina — as light steadies, dips.

Outings 1 — The Thames

The places you want to go!
   The Thames by bus —

sun throwing linked shapes
   as we lean on fluid time

and melt, as cloud
   turns the river to dark glass

and, later, the sun projects each leaf
   again, softens rough skin…

Our arms link — see, twinned!
   and, on numb current, floating.

Outings II — Shopping

Behind the stairs — best place
   on the bus — bodies
     close and warm.

Simply *bronking* on that bus,
   simply going shopping,
     met pain

with London thrills —
   the moon's loose cannon
     crashing

blank windows
   above yellow shops
     Madonna-

blue sky torn
   to rags, clouds blown
     like brown ashes.

Outings III — Follow that Cab

The photo, pre-cancer,
  shows *resistance* —

wide *Plath* mouth,
  hair gilt from a bottle

a dream of pleasure floats
  on your face. Too weak to cross

London (I thought) you told drivers,
  'I've no time'

and cabbies showed true grit,
  raced for the Kilburn *Salon*.

Translating Horace in Landells Road

Ice glitters the heels
  of streams in spate —
    Summer's

shade darkens,
  sinks to stream-beds,
    new ice creeps out...

We come this way
  once... 'Is that
    good English?'

Outside, bare felloes
  of rush-hour
    shake the house —

later, the traffic
  calms. 'Something
    still left out!'

The Hospice Makes an Error

You shared a bedroom
    with two *coffins,*

moribund, in coma —
    daughters weeping all night…

came home sleepless,
    we sat in the dark, still riled,

grew calm talking of things
    tenderly indifferent,

attuned to any presence
    here, trying to forgive.

Fish Man

Tumours bulged your thin body,
    breasts were flat pockets
        on a school-dress of the past.

He cheered Fridays, immensely,
    left Hastings at 5am,
        one Shakespeare earring…

'Dying.' The fish man's bright cleaver
    threw in the trimmings —
        'Simmer. Very good.'

Three nights a week, night-club bouncer
    paid off the mortgage. You
        sucked hope from his bones.

Cooking Fish Chowder

In this *bain-marie,* Death won't find us.
  Your face in steam like a yashmak...

why squabble, though? I won't dispute
  recipes but open my hands...

You dive for tongue's memories —
  chillies, limes, fennel, even spuds...

Tented in fragrant broth, 'Good!'
  beads of ice melt from our eyes.

Haworth — the Bronte Sofa

When I saw it as a child, the obstacle
  stuck against thin North light —

sofa, horse-hair in the darkest cloth...
  On a chaise-longue of steel and black calf

you're trapped in the upper room
  with one *helper* who asked, 'When is it due?'

You laugh — 'How old am I? But she's right,
  growing each day'. Like *galloping consumption.*

Flowers I

As I darkened your house, friends' flowers
  closed in, obeyed Nature, the engineer,
    who tunes petals to light-values

but won't crimp petals of thought,
  close glaring grids of fear...
    In two hours, you stretch a hand

to dope again... Poppies sway false drowse,
    words spill from your mind's confused retort,
    which in my house I seem to hear, 'No!'

Flowers II

We call for a spaceship for the soul —
    small seed, catapulted, wind borne.

Lilies that fester...
    Shakespeare's hard words. Hopes darken

from doped dreams. With too much haste
    (a lily gone soft at the root)

thought corrupts sense and perfumes we detect
    are composition, office of fire, last forms.

Flowers III

A florist-shop of blooms
    marked the bed — your son
        drowsed over your held hand.

I took the other... Your voice filled
    word-shapes slowly, spoke in colours —
        'Stunning red petals!'

Not here, in your dream. We're blind
    to your Tiger, who pads up,
        'Look! Abricot and black!'

Goodbye

I close the London A–Z. The church
  seems unconnected with your life —
    perhaps this fits?

'Small house of unobstructed light'*
  The route, dog-leg, needs no highlight
    in the book — do it blind!

But in there, on your page, I've biro'd
  all the streets between us red.

**from Veronica's poem, 'Epithalamion at King's Cross'*

Notes on contributors & acknowledgments to publishers

DANNIE ABSE is a Fellow of the Royal Society of Literature and President of The Welsh Academy of Letters. His *New and Collected Poems* is published by Hutchinson (2003)

SHANTA ACHARYA's two collections of poetry are *Not This, Not That* (Rupa, 1994) and *Numbering Our Days' Illusions* (Rockingham Press, 1995). Her study, *The Influence of Indian Thought on Ralph Waldo Emerson*, was published by The Edwin Mellen Press in 2001.

TIMOTHY ADÈS is a poetry translator, often working with rhyme. In 2002 his first book, Victor Hugo's *How to be a Grandfather* (Hearing Eye) appeared and also his translation of poems by Jean Cassou (Arc Visible Poets).

JOHN ARDEN, Playwright and novelist, was born in Barnsley, Yorkshire in 1930, has lived in Ireland since the 1960s. Works include: plays — *Serjeant Musgrave's Dance*, 1959; *The Non-Stop Connolly Show*, written with Margaretta D'Arcy, 1975: novels — *Jack Juggler*, 1995.

PAT ARROWSMITH, pacifist and socialist. Amnesty International staff member 24 years. Political prisoner 11 times. Several collections of poems and drawings including *Drawing to Extinction* (Hearing Eye, 2000). Has also published novels and memoirs. **War in Afghanistan** appeared in *Nonviolent Action*.

WANDA BARFORD, on retiring from teaching music, decided to put poetry at the centre of her life. 3 collections published by Flambard: *Sweet Wine and Bitter Herbs, A Moon at the Door* and *Losing, Finding*. **You left Paris first** appeared in *Acumen*.

BRUCE BARNES works for a mental health charity in Bradford and also as a freelance poet/performer. He prefers the capriciousness of the poetry competition to occasional appearances in poetry magazines. His second collection *Somewhere Else* was published in 2002.

MICHAEL BARTHOLOMEW-BIGGS is a mathematician by day and a poet at other times. His first collection *Anglicized by Common Use* appeared in 1998 (Waldean Press). A second, *Inklings of Complicity* is due from Pikestaff Press in 2003.

GERARD BENSON, London born, toured, recorded and performed with the Barrow Poets. He is part of the *Poems on the Underground* team and has been poet-in-residence at The Wordsworth Trust. His latest book is *To catch an elephant*, new and collected verse for children, (Smith Doorstop, 2002). **Bionic** was published in *The North, 1998.*

OLIVER BERNARD was born in 1925. Poet and translator of *Apollinaire* (Anvil) and *Rimbaud, Collected Poems* (Penguin Classics). His third collection is *Verse &c.* (Anvil, 2001). *Getting Over It* (Peter Owen, 1992) is an autobiography.

JO BIDDER, writer and poet, is a founder and former Director of Survivors' Poetry which promotes poetry by survivors of mental distress, and is Chair of the Arts Council of England's Art and Disability Advisory Panel. **Sun and Stucco** was published in *Acumen, spring 1999*, **Rainham Cemetery** and **Apple Blossom** in *Matter of Life and Death, Zzero, 1990*.

PAUL BIRTILL was born in Walton, Liverpool in 1960, but now lives in London. His poems appear regularly in national newspapers and literary magazines. He also writes plays, one of which was shortlisted for the Verity Bargate Award.

SARA BOYES has published two collections of poetry, *Kite* and *Wild Flowers* and has edited *Frankenstein's Daughter,* an anthology of women's poetry. She has co-devised poetry and music events including *My Cat Geoffrey,* performed at Torriano. She teaches creative writing in Islington and at Birkbeck.

ALAN BROWNJOHN's books include two *Collected Poems* and *The Cat Without E-mail* (2001). His latest novel was *A Funny Old Year* (2001). **Found Object** and **An Alteration** are from a privately-circulated, extempore millenium poem entitled *Two Thousand and One.*

DAVID BRYANT was born in Ilford and raised in Southend, but has spent most of his adult life in Portsmouth. He currently resides in East London and has been active on the spoken word circuit for eight years.

PETER CAMPBELL was born and raised in Scotland. He now lives in Cricklewood, North West London. He is a founder member of Survivors' Poetry and has produced two collections of poems: *In Two Worlds* and *The Way It Feels.*

JULIA CASTERTON writes and teaches in London. She has three collections of poems and *Creative Writing – A Practical Guide* (Palgrave). **Here is the room** was published in *Ambit.*

ALAN CHAMBERS' latest book, *Ordered Lines* was published by The Stonemark Press in 2000. Formerly Artistic Director of Questors Theatre, he has had translations and revues performed here and in the USA. Obsessions are the sea and small boats.

RUTH CHRISTIE for many years has taught English Literature and translated Turkish poetry, novels and stories. *Voices of Memory* (Rockingham Press) is a selection of Oktay Rifat poems translated by Ruth Christie and Richard McKane.

JOHN E. CLARKE lives in Leyton and works in Stepney for Tower Hamlets Education as a mentor. Poems in FIRE, still and Presence and has written a first play 'Giving as the world gives'. **The Dictionary** was published in *The Affectionate Punch* (2000).

JOHN R. CLARKE, inveterate S.E. Londoner, regular reader/performer on London's spoken word circuit. Debut collection *Travelling Without Arriving* (The Tall Lighthouse,2001). A chapbook *Jazz and Other Religions* is out in 2003.

JEFF CLOVES, poet, hack, self-publisher. Would prefer to have played football for Spurs.

MARGARETTA D'ARCY. Irish. Playwright and multi-media worker. Human rights activist. Member of Aosdána (Irish artists' parliament). Lives in Galway and runs Radio Pirate-Woman, one of the world's smallest broadcasting stations.

SIMON DARRAGH moved from England to Greece when Thatcher got in; then there was Major, then Blair, so he's still living on Alonnisos, a small island in the Aegean, where he rebuilds motorbikes, plays saxophone, trumpet, clarinet, guitar and bouzouki, fixes people's plumbing and produces a weekly A4 English language newsheet.

ADÈLE DAVID is an artist and Jungian Training Analyst and Supervisor. Winner of a Caernarvon Festival prize and the Cheltenham Festival Appleby Cup, she has published widely in various magazines and anthologies. Her second collection of poems *The Moon's Song* is published by Katabasis.

SUSAN DE MUTH, writer and translator, lives and sometimes works in London. In 2002, Hearing Eye published her translation of Elsa Triolet's *Mayakovsky – Russian Poet, A Memoir 1939*; this includes new versions of some of Mayakovsky's poems.

BOB DEVEREUX is a poet, painter and director of the Salthouse Gallery, St. Ives, Cornwall. Publications include *Be Green* (Ark Press) and *The Little Book of Moon Poems* (Lapwing Press). As a librettist he has written the text for eight operas and worked with nine composers.

BRIAN DOCHERTY, born in Glasgow, now lives in north London. Widely published in magazines & anthologies. First collection *Armchair Theatre* published by Hearing Eye in 1999. A second book, *A Desk With A View*, is forthcoming. **Cheers** published in *Incognito*.

BEATA DUNCAN has taught English Literature to students from nine to ninety. Worked in publishing and as a researcher. Poems anthologized and widely published in magazines. Small collection *Apple Harvest* (Hearing Eye). Lives in North London. **Problem page** published in *Rialto*, **Crane Beach** in *London Magazine*.

JANE DURAN, born in Cuba, brought up in the United States and Chile, has lived in England since 1966. Publications: *Boogie Woogie* (Hearing Eye, 1991); *Breathe Now, Breathe* (Enitharmon, 1995) – Forward Poetry Prize for Best First Collection and *Silences from the Spanish Civil War* (Enitharmon, 2002). **Coastal** and **There are Women** published in *Poetry Review* and then in *La Generación del Cordero, Trilce Ediciones, Mexico, 2000*.

ANTHONY EDKINS, born in Cheshire in 1927. Has lived in Madrid, San Francisco, New York and London. Latest poetry collections: *The Exile* (Hearing Eye, 2001) and *Life As It Comes* (Redbeck, 2002). Translations from Spanish include two novels by Javier Tomeo (Carcanet, 1991) and poems by Rafael Alberti, Luis Cernuda, Manuel Machado and Cesar Vallejo.

JANE ELDER was born in the Isle of Man, read Classics at Cambridge, taught Classics and English in the London area. Her translation of Seneca's *Thyestes* won an EE Translation Competition (Mid Northumberland Arts Group/Carcanet Press) and was broadcast on Radio 3.

DAVID ELIOT has had work published in Tower Hamlets Arts Project anthologies and has read widely on the London poetry circuit.

FLORENCE ELON divides her time between England and America. Has taught creative writing and literature at the University of California (Berkeley); as Visiting Writer: Northwestern, Yale. Poems published by Chatto, the Keepsake, Phoenix, Sceptre Presses, Secker, anthologies and journals.

JANE FRASER ESSON has worked as a journalist, read English at Birkbeck College, London. Three poetry collections, the latest *The Magenta Café* (Hub Editions, 2000). She also writes fiction.

MARTINA EVANS grew up in Ireland and moved to London in 1988. She is the author of two books of poetry and three novels, the latest of which is *No Drinking No Dancing No Doctors* (Bloomsbury, 2000). At present she is completing her fourth novel and teaches Creative Writing at the City Lit.

HARRY EYRES was born in London in 1958 and lives in Brixton. He was Poetry Editor of the Daily Express from 1996 to 2001. His first collection *Hotel Eliseo* was published by Hearing Eye. He was a Whitbread Poetry Award judge in 2001.

SHELAH FLOREY was brought up in London. She has been published in *Poetry Introduction 8* (Faber and Faber) and in various anthologies including *Work* (Katabasis). Her collection *The Making of Casablanca* was published by Hearing Eye in 1999. She has received a London Writers Award.

DAVID FLOYD was born in north London in 1980. Former film critic for *Morning Star* and library assistant at the University of North London, currently editor of the award-winning youth magazine *Exposure*. His *War in the Playground* is Torriano Meeting House Poetry Pamphlet No. 32.

NIGEL FOXELL was born in London in 1931. As well as writing poetry, he has translated French, German and Italian poets. He has also written *Ten Poems Analysed* (Pergamon, 1973) and *A Sermon in Stone* (Menard, 1978) – about John Donne. His novel *The Marriage Seat* (Harvester, 1973) was a New Fiction Society Choice.

LEAH FRITZ has lived long enough to doubt nearly everything, and this fluidity of mind/spirit is reflected in her three collections of poetry. A quintessential New Yorker, she unreservedly blesses the sea change that brought her to London in 1985.

KATHERINE GALLAGHER's collections include *Fish-rings on Water* (Forest, 1989), *Finding the Prince* (Hearing Eye, 1993) and *Tigers on the Silk Road* (Arc Publications, 2000). Runner-up in the 2000 *Stand* Poetry Competition. Currently Writer-in-Residence at Railway Fields Nature Reserve, Haringey. **Gwen John** appeared in *Mslexia*, **Thinking of my mother** in *Lancaster Festival Anthology, 1996*.

DONALD GARDNER has been writing and performing poetry since the 1960s. A Londoner, he now lives in Amsterdam where he works as a translator. His recent book of poems is *How to get the most out of your Jet Lag* (New Haven, 2001). **Octopus** appeared in *Ambit*.

RAYMOND GEUSS, born 1946, teaches philosophy at Cambridge and is the author of *Parrots, poets, philosophers, and good advice* and *At Cross Purposes* (both Hearing Eye). He has also published various monographs on political philosophy.

JOHN GODFREY is a former railway manager. Published in a number of magazines; competition successes include **Big Sur Café** 1st prize, Kent & Sussex, **The Permanent Way**, 1st prize, Chiltern Writers, also Bridport and

Ver Poets competitions. He lives in Hitchin and doesn't write as much as he'd like.

MIRIAM HALAHMY was born in London in 1952. She has published a poetry collection *Stir Crazy* (Hub Editions, 1994) and a novel *Secret Territory* (Citron Press, 1999). Her second poetry collection *Cutting Pomegranates* is published in 2003. Washing Apples appeared in *The Dybbuk of Delight*.

DAVID HALLIWELL, playwright, is the author of *Little Malcolm and his Struggle against the Eunuchs*. A playscript, *One Sez This Then The Other Sez That, Extracts From a Work in Progress* will be published by Hearing Eye. He is writing *Turning Aperture Appendage Situations Turning* for the Bush Theatre.

LUCY HAMILTON started writing poetry when she joined the Poetry School in 1998. Poems published in *Psychopoetica, Staple, Smiths Knoll, The Interpreter's House* and in two anthologies: *Parents* (Enitharmon, 2000) and *Making Worlds* (Headland Press).

CHRISTOPHER HAMPTON taught English in Rome and for 27 years at the Polytechnic of Central London. As well as three volumes of poems, publications include *The Etruscans* (Gollancz), *Socialism in a Crippled World* and *A Radical Reader* (Penguin). Has recently completed a novel, a book of poems and one of critical essays, *Border Crossings*.

CARLTON HARDY's work includes poems showing concern for human problems and he believes that if poetry can't change the world, it can raise sympathetic awareness. His imaginative work is drawn from life's lucky – or unlucky – dip.

MELISSA HARMAN wrote poetry as a child and young adult but put artistic creativity into a closet for years while working in journalism and grappling with the often discordant lyricism of growing up and motherhood.

JAMES HARVEY studied Biology at university, concentrating on Ecology. After leaving university he decided to concentrate on poetry. He has poems in *Brittle Star* magazine and in *Poetry Salzburg Review.*

MARIA HEATH was born in 1967, and grew up in Yorkshire. She went briefly to the University of East Anglia, left to live in Paris as a poet and artist and subsequently studied theology, philosophy and art at London colleges. She has three children.

JOHN HEATH-STUBBS was born in London in 1918, educated in Hampshire, Sussex and the Isle of Wight obtaining first class honours in English Literature at Queen's College, Oxford. First poems in wartime volume *Eight Oxford Poets*. Received Queen's Gold Medal for Poetry in 1958 and later on, OBE for services to literature. His poor eyesight, diagnosed at the age of three, deteriorated to total blindness in his adult life. Published seven pamphlets with Hearing Eye. His current book from his main publisher Carcanet is *The Return of the Cranes.*

JOHN HEGLEY was born in Islington, to which London borough he has returned. He has books published by Deutsch and Methuen and a recent children's book *My Dog is a Carrot* (Walker). He first performed at Torriano in the mid-eighties with Brown Paper Bag Brothers.

CICELY HERBERT is a co-founder of *Poems on the Underground* and a Barrow Poet. Poetry includes *In Hospital* (Katabasis). She has written and performed several concert pieces with music by Jim Parker. Co-author with Ann Langton of *87, Holmes Road, the story of one building's contribution to the life of Kentish Town: London Board School to Camden Institute.*

DANIELLE HOPE has two poetry collections, *Fairground of Madness* and *City Fox*, and a third, *The Stone Ship*, appearing in spring 2003 (all Rockingham Press). She is an advisory editor of *Acumen* magazine, and an advisor to *Survivors Poetry.*

SUE HUBBARD, poet, novelist, art critic, a founder of Blue Nose poets. Books include *Everything Begins with the Skin* (Enitharmon) and a novel *Depth of Field* (Dewi Lewis) and she has newer poems in *Oxford Poets 2000* (Carcanet). An Arts Council-commissioned poem is stencilled along an underpass at the South Bank, London.

CAROL HUGHES is a Canadian living in London. She has taught various subjects including Chinese art history and English as a foreign language. She began writing and painting in her 50s and has published some poetry and fiction.

MIROSLAV JANCIC was born in Sarajevo, secured a tomb there too. He's lived there all the time, spending some years abroad. Curiously enough, in the rest of the meantime he keeps himself together mainly with the help of English.

ROLAND JOHN's poems, criticism and reviews have appeared in most UK literary journals. Available poetry collections are *Believing Words are Real* (Agenda Editions) and *To Weigh Alternatives* (Headland). Other books include *A Beginner's Guide to The Cantos of Ezra Pound* (Hippopotamus) and *A Choice of Poets* (Hodder). **History** appeared in *The Poet's Voice*, **Fish market** in *Agenda.*

JENNIFER JOHNSON was born in Bakht-er-Ruda, Sudan. Has worked as an agriculturalist in Zambia. Now publications assistant for the History of Parliament Trust. Runs the Spinning Room poetry group in London. Two collections *Stinging Nettles* and *Erasing My Footprints* (both Nettle Press).

JEANETTE JU-PIERRE began writing poetry in 1971 when she was in St. Lucia, composing romantic poems in paradise. In the early nineties the Caribbean voice emerged. Publications are *The Hibiscus Collection* (Ed Phelps, Canada, 1984) and *Crushed Calabash* (Hearing Eye, 1994).

MARTHA KAPOS is an American living in London. In 2002 she was included in Carcanet's *Oxford Poets Anthology*. Her first collection is *My Nights in Cupid's Palace* (Enitharmon, 2003). She is Assistant Poetry Editor of *Poetry London.*

JUDITH KAZANTZIS has published eight and more poetry collections, including her *Selected Poems, The Odysseus Poems* (1999) and *Swimming Through The Grand Hotel* (1997). Her first novel is *Of Love and Terror* (Saqi, 2002). She lives in Lewes. **Sunshine** appeared in *Ambit, 2000,* **The woods of Balacet** in *Writing Women, 1993,* **After a lifetime together...** in *Poetry Wales, 1999.*

DAN KENNEDY, Kilkenny-born performance poet and singer. Has been coming to Torriano poetry evenings for 10 years. Dreamer, crier, storyteller, Dan has produced a CD *Songs from a fierce head* and, more recently, a collection of poems, now ready for publication.

JOHN (JOHANNES) KERKHOVEN was born in Holland. Lived in Australia, 1954-79 and London since 1979. Retired compositor, graphic artist/photographer, BA Eng. Lit., Birkbeck. Has published poems in *Literary Review* and *Connections*, short stories, travel articles and photographs in UK and Australia. **Blossom** appeared in *Connections* Winter 99/2000.

MIMI KHALVATI was born in Tehran and grew up on the Isle of Wight. She has worked as an actor and director in the UK and Iran. Her published works include *In White Ink, Mirrorwork, Entries on Light, Selected Poems* and *The Chine* (all Carcanet). She is founder and co-ordinator of the Poetry School, which offers poetry workshops and courses in London.

ANGELA KIRBY was born in Lancashire in 1932. She has five children and has worked as a chef, gardener, garden designer, author and freelance journalist. Published in various magazines and anthologies. Has won a handful of prizes including BBC Wildlife Poet of the Year in 1995 and 2001.

BERNARD KOPS, poet, novelist and playwright, was born in the East End of London in 1926 of Jewish Dutch working class parents. His first play was *The Hamlet of Stepney Green*. He published two books of poetry with Hearing Eye *Barricades in West Hampstead* (1989) and *Grandchildren and other poems* (2000). His autobiography *The World is a Wedding* was continued in *Shalom Bomb* (2000).

LOTTE KRAMER came to England as a refugee child in 1939, lost her parents and family in Shoah. Engaged in all kinds of work while studying Art/History of Art in evening classes. Exhibitions. Began to write in the 1970s. Published nine volumes of poetry, the most recent *The Phantom Lane* (Rockingham) and *Selected and New Poems 1980-1997*. **Exodus** appeared in *Acumen*, **Ex-India, 1940s** in *Ambit*, **Library men** in *Leviathan* and as a *Ver Poets poem card*.

PHILIPPA LAWRENCE worked in the theatre and television, then pioneered restoring textiles in stately homes. Losing her voice and reciting poetry as therapy inspired her to take courses. She has won prizes, and been published in anthologies, magazines and newspapers.

SARAH LAWSON was born in Indianapolis in 1943 but has lived in London since 1969. She has taught at Suzhou University in China and lectured on British poetry in three other provinces. She has translated Christine de Pisan's *Treasure of the City of Ladies* (Penguin) and *Jacques Prévert: Selected Poems* for Hearing Eye.

MARGARET LEFF was born in Haifa 193... 'I am still alive! I enjoy a glass of wine with friends and travelling to non-exotic places, in cramped style. I have worked in Italy & Africa. and now live happily in Kentish Town'. Has read her *Dorothea Quarry* poems at Torriano and on Welsh Television.

EDDIE LINDEN. Scots-Irish, born Ireland of Irish parents, grew up Scotland. Poet, founder in 1969 and editor of the literary magazine *Aquarius*. Publications: *City of Razors* (1980) poems; *Who is Eddie Linden?* a biography (with Sebastian Barker, 1979), adapted for stage by William Tanner (London, 1997). Poems in anthologies *The Best of Scottish Poetry* (1989), *Life Doesn't Frighten Me At All* (1989), *The Poolbeg Book of Irish Poetry* (1997). Has read on radio and television.

DINAH LIVINGSTONE has lived in Camden Town since 1966 and has been reading at Torriano since its early days. Nine pamphlets, five books of poetry, including *Time on Earth: Selected and New Poems* (Rockingham, 1999). Latest translation: Subcomandante Marcos' *Zapatista Stories* (Katabasis, 2001).

ALEXIS LYKIARD lives in Exeter. Most recent prose book *Jean Rhys Revisited* (Stride, 2000). Other publications include poetry, novels and translations. Creation Books publish his version of Artaud's *Heliogabalus* in 2003, when a new poetry collection, *Skeleton Keys* (Redback) also appears.

THOMAS MCCOLL was born in 1970 and lives in London. He regularly reads at various poetry venues in London including Torriano. Works in the book trade.

SUE MACINTYRE has been a book editor all her working life. Now retired, she is increasingly concentrating on writing poetry. Her work has appeared in the anthology *Parents* (Enitharmon/Second Light). She has written a sequence, *Peter*, drawing on her father's letters. A pamphlet *Picnic with Sea Fog and Elephants* is published by the Many Press in 2003.

RICHARD MCKANE, poet, and translator of over 25 books from Russian and Turkish including Akhmatova, Mandelstam, Nazim Hikmet and Oktay Rifat (the last two with Ruth Christie). *Poet for Poet* (Hearing Eye, 1998 reprinted 2001) contains his own poems and his best-loved translations. He is an interpreter at the Medical Foundation for the Care of Victims of Torture.

KATHLEEN MCPHILEMY was born in Northern Ireland but has lived in Britain for many years. She has published two books of poetry *Witness to Magic* (Hearing Eye, 1990) and *A Tented Peace* (Katabasis, 1995) and a number of pamphlets.

E.A. MARKHAM, Professor of Creative Writing at Sheffield Hallam University. Edited *Hinterland* (The Bloodaxe Book of Caribbean poetry). In 2002 he published *A Rough Climate* (Anvil) – his seventh collection of poems – and *Taking the Drawing Room through Customs: Selected Stories* (Peepal Tree). Forthcoming *Selected Poems* (Salt, Australia).

JEHANE MARKHAM lives in Kentish Town. She first read at Torriano Meeting House with her mother, Olive Dehn, in 1994. Publications include *20 Poems* (1999) and *My Mother Myself* (2001) an audio tape, (both Rough Winds Productions).

NANCY MATTSON, a Western Canadian in London since 1990, has had many publications on both sides of the Atlantic. *Maria Breaks Her Silence* (Regina: Coteau, 1989) was shortlisted for best first collection of poetry in Canada. **Ceremony of Eels** published in *The Interpreter's House 16*, (2001).

GERDA MAYER was born in Karlsbad, Czechoslovakia and came to England in 1939 at the age of eleven. **Snapshots** will be in her collection *Hoppickers' Holiday*, due from Happy Dragons Press in 2003. She has been previously published by Chatto & Windus, Ceolfrith Press, O.U.P. (for children), Priapus Press, Peterloo Poets, Hearing Eye and Iron Press. **Don't**

Give a Fairy the Cold Shoulder was in *Go and Open the Door*, Macmillan Educational, *1987*, **Young man leaning...** in *Rosalia, a Manifold anthology, 2001*.
MARY MICHAELS is the author of five pamphlet collections. A volume of new and selected poems *The Shape of the Rock* is to be published by Sea Cow in 2003.
JOAN MICHELSON was born in Boston, Massachusetts and now lives in London. A recent publication is *Letting in the Light: a journey through grief* (Poetic Matrix Press, CA, USA); writing fellowships: Virginia Center for the Creative Arts, VA. '02, Djerassi Resident Arts Program, California '03.
DAVID MILLER's publications include *W.H. Hudson and the Elusive Paradise* (Macmillan), *Pictures of Mercy* (Stride), *Art and Disclosure* (Stride) and *Spiritual Letters (1-12)* (hawkhaven press). His work has been anthologised in *The New British Poetry, 1968 – 1988* (Paladin Books). **Poem** appeared in *Acumen* and *Lutherans in London*, **Spiritual letters** in *Shearsman.*
C.D. MORGAN, born 1944, Hammersmith – rural childhood – worked as a clerk – joined small literary group – returned to London in 1967 – fringe politics led to work as playleader – became teacher 1975 for 17 years – began writing again in the '90s.
SHARON MORRIS trained as a visual artist and has exhibited photography, film and video based on her prose poems. Her poetry has appeared in *Coil, Other Poetry, Envoi, Poetry Salzburg Review* and the anthologies *Her Mind's Eye* and *Tying the Song.*
ROSEMARY NORMAN is one of Michael Horowitz's *Grandchildren of Albion.* She has published two collections *Threats and Promises* (Iron Press, 1991) and *Life on Mars* (Hearing Eye, 1999), the latter being accompanied by a video by Stuart Pound. She works as a librarian.
NICK ORENGO was born in 1956, educated at Dulwich College and Essex University. Publications: *Let the dead sing* (Semantron Press), *Bright in Imagined Numbers* (Hearing Eye). Has worked as an artist and pianist. Won second prize in Manchester Cathedral Poetry Competition 2001.
WILLIAM OXLEY was born in Manchester. A poet and philosopher, he has also worked as accountant, part-time gardener and actor. Lives in South Devon. Founder of the Long Poem Group, he co-edits its newsletter. Rockingham Press published his autobiography *No Accounting for Paradise* (1999) and *Reclaiming the Lyre: New and Selected Poems* (2001).
MARY PARKER *Biographical-details:* paint/ write/ play the guitar and growl to/ the music as best/ I can.
LINDA ROSE PARKES was born in Jersey, studied at the University of East Anglia, lived and worked in Germany for twenty years, giving her first London reading at Torriano in 1992. Has been widely published in magazines and anthologies. Has now returned to Jersey.
PERSE PEETT worked as a schoolteacher and as a puppeteer after having a very varied career including restoration stonemason. He now spends his time telling traditional stories with music and singing folksongs.
JEAN PESTELL was educated in England and France, has lived in Spain. Trilingual, taught English/French at the British-American Institute, Madrid. Currently archivist. Married to an author, with two children.

MARIO PETRUCCI, physicist, ecologist, songwriter, educator, poet. Literacy consultant at the Imperial War Museum and its first poet-in-residence. Winner of the Arvon International Poetry Competition (2002) and an Arts Council Writers' Award for forthcoming *Flowers of Sulphur* (Enitharmon, 2004). Hearing Eye published a long ecological poem *Bosco* .

PETER PHILLIPS' pamphlet *Frayed At The Edges* was published in 1997 and his first full collection *Looking For You* in 2001 (both Hearing Eye).

PHIL POOLE was born in 1944 in Birmingham. Graduated in English in 1967 as an external student. Took up sculpture. Presently employed by Parliamentary Work Directorate as restorer of woodcarving designed by Pugin. Earlier interest in poetry became more intense around 1998.

HILARY PORTER was born in Horsham, Sussex in 1943. She has been involved in various poetry groups for more than twenty years and was a founder member of Survivors' Poetry. She is a mother and grandmother, and also draws inspiration from art, astrology and travel.

FRANCES PRESLEY lives and works in London. She has written essays and reviews about innovative poetry, particularly by British women poets. Publications include: *Neither the one nor the other* with the poet Elizabeth James (Form Books, 1999; also on CD); *Automatic cross stitch* with the artist Irma Irsara (Other Press, 2000) and *Somerset Letters* (Oasis, 2002).

JEREMY REED has published over forty books of poetry, fiction and non-fiction. His most recent, a 250 page poem on Elvis Presley *Heartbreak Hotel* is published by Orion. A Somerset Maugham Award winner.

ROBERTO RIVERA-REYES was born in 1953 in Chile, fleeing after the military coup overthrew Allende in 1973. He has lived in England since 1974 and now runs the Latin American Cultural Institute in London. *Dawn Hunters and Other Poems* (1989) and *Anthology of Latin American Poets in London* (editor, 1988) are both bilingual productions by Latin American Writers Publications). **The Trees Sing like Rivers** is in *Mother Tongues: Modern Poetry in Translation 17* (King's College London, 2001).

JO ROACH, a founder member of *All mouth no trousers* – a literary cabaret. An organiser of *Poetry and Jazz* at the Poetry Café, Covent Garden and organiser of *Poetry Street* as part of the Stoke Newington Festival.

ANNA ROBINSON lives in south London. She works in H.M.P. Brixton's library with prisoner-poets and others. She has been published in various journals/anthologies. In 2001 she was awarded a Poetry School Scholarship (supported by London Arts). **What the Water Gave Anna** was in *Poetry Street, 2001.*

TOM RUBENS has spent most of his working life as a teacher of English, both in this country and abroad. He has poems in anthologies and has published three books on philosophy, and has written a novel. A humanist, he was editor of *The Ethical Record* for several years.

MYRA SCHNEIDER's most recent collection is *Insisting on Yellow: new and selected poems* (Enitharmon, 2000). *Writing My Way Through Cancer* – a fleshed-out journal with writing notes and poems, is due in 2003 (Jessica Kingsley). She tutors for The Poetry School. **Amazon** appeared in *Poetry London*, **Orange Trees of Seville** in *Foolscap Chapbook Series, 2001*, **Piano** in *Aireings.*

GAVIN SELERIE was born in London in 1949. He teaches at the Faculty of Continuing Education, University of London. His books include *Azimuth* (1984), *Roxy* (1996) and *Days of '49* (1999). The poems included here are from a work in progress, *Le Fanu's Ghost*, a gothic text involving both poetry and prose.

BILL SHERMAN is the only American ever to hold simultaneous residency status for both Britain and for the islands of French Polynesia. In 1990 he published *Tahitian Journals* (Hearing Eye). Segments of his latest book *Of Rapa Nui* are published in the poetry journals *Fire* and *Spanner*.**The Storehouse of Imperialist Theft** published in *Fire*.

LABI SIFFRE has volumes of poetry on the web including *A Hope in Hell* and *Breaking the Bloody Glass*; books *Nigger, Blood on the Page* and *Monument*; a play *Deathwrite*; essays *Letters from an Alien* and the song *Something Inside So Strong*.

DENNIS SIMMONS the eminent (he says) lives nowadays at Maidstone – or exists with difficulty. Still has copies of his 1995 pamphlet *Alright By My Friends* – available (worth £350 per copy someone said) to anyone who has won the lottery.

JANET SIMON is a previous prizewinner in the National Poetry Competition. Her collection *Victoria Park* is published by Loxwood Stoneleigh. She is currently preparing a new book to be called *King Harvest*. She lives and works in London.

HYLDA SIMS writes novels, poetry and songs. One of the prime movers in the skiffle era. Her novel *Inspecting the Island* based on Summerhill School, where she was educated, was published in 2000. She lives in South London and co-runs *Poetry & Jazz* at the Poetry Café in Covent Garden, London.

RUTH SMITH's poems have appeared in several magazines and anthologies including Faber and Faber's *First Pressings*. In 1996 she won the London Writers' Poetry Prize. She used to teach English in a secondary school but now gives her time to writing.

EMILY TAYLOR comes from a farming background in County Galway, Ireland and has lived in London since 1988. She has always maintained her two passions, painting and writing, and has had several exhibitions and publications during her time here.

ALYSON TORNS works as a tennis coach in Hertfordshire and is currently doing a degree in Creative Writing at Luton University. She has had poems published in *Poetry London, The Interpreter's House, Fire* and *Poetry Salzburg Review* and has read at various London poetry venues.

CHRISTOPHER TRUMAN was born in Taiping, Malaysia during the anti-Communist 'Emergency'. He travelled extensively in *Mitteleuropa* before the end of the Cold War. He was the only Englishman on the first civilian flight between Warsaw and Vilnius since 1939. The poems here are all from a work in progress, *Parallel Cold:* an early version of **Insomnia '82** was in *Orbis No. 74, Autumn 1989*.

CHRISTOPHER TWIGG was born in Bromsgrove in 1958. First collection *In the Choir* (Alces Press, 1997), was *The Guardian*'s Paperback of the Week . Read his work on Radio 4's 'Poetry Please' and has appeared in Channel 4's 'Litpop' series. Travelled to Chile in January 2000 where, by good fortune, he met Nicanor Parra.

DUBRAVKA VELASEVIC was born in Montenegro, where she worked as a medical doctor until 1992 when she arrived in London where she currently lives. She has published five books of poetry, two of them in English - *Farewell Montenegro* and *Sleeping Volcano* (Hearing Eye).

CRISTINA VITI is a translator published in *Modern Poetry in Translation* and by Brindin Press. Her poems featured in the *Poetry Street* festival.

JENNY VUGLAR was born in New Zealand but has lived in London since 1979. Her poetry and plays have been widely published and performed. **The Underwriter from Lloyds** published in *The Interpreter's House*, **Fox** in *Second Light Newsletter*, **Northland** in *Rialto*.

STEPHEN WATTS born 1952 London, mother's family from Swiss-Italian Alps. Poet: *The Lava's Curl* (1990 rpr. 2002), *Gramsci & Caruso: Selected Poems* (2002), two chapbook long poems *Praha Poem* & *Birds of East London*. Editor (*Mother Tongues*, 2001) and translator/researcher. Now working on essays, prose pieces and a book of long poems. Enough & not enough!

PAT V.T. WEST. performer of feminist/confessional poems since the seventies, of monologue pieces in character since the nineties; member *Riff Raff Poets*; creative writing tutor, organiser *Poetry & Words* (Glastonbury Festival) & *Rive Gauche Poetry* (Bristol).

BRENDA WILLIAMS, protest poet, was born in Leeds in 1948. Recently, she has concentrated on writing poems that highlight the plight of mental health patients, both locally and nationally.

RAY WILLMOTT was born in London. He has published poetry in the anthologies *Under the Asylum Tree* (1995) and *Beyond Bedlam* (Anvil, 1997). First collection *Easier Dead Than Son* (Nettle Press, 1998).

DILYS WOOD studied English at Cambridge and served 20 years hard labour in the Civil Service before returning to poetry; *Women Come to a Death* was published by Katabasis, 1997. She runs the Second Light Network for older women poets. Veronica Rospigliosi, the subject of the sequence **Veronica**, died at Christmas 1999. *Reckitt's Blue*, a small collection of poems by Veronica, was published in November 1999 by Hearing Eye.